Merry Christmas
Rachel!

+

CORINTHIAN RESOLVE

The Story of the Marion-Bermuda Race

CORINTHIAN RESOLVE

The Story of the Marion-Bermuda Race

MARK J. GABRIELSON

Published by the
Marion-Bermuda Cruising Yacht Race Association, Inc.
www.marionbermuda.com

First published in 2017

Manufactured in the United States

ISBN   978-0-99739-204-3

Book Design: Claire MacMaster, barefoot art graphic design

Celestial class
competitors
Wayward Wind
(left) and *Patriot*
departing Buzzards
Bay downwind in
the 2003 race.
Photo: Fran Grenon

This book is dedicated to my Marion-Bermuda Race crew:
Steve Bussolari, Mark DeVine, Al Larkin,
Lisa Gabrielson McCurdy, and Dave Patton.
Lyra *couldn't have done it without you.*

Two Chesapeake Bay boats at work. The Navy 44 *Swift* and Bob Anderson's *Ariel* in close quarters in pre-race maneuvers before the 2015 race. *Swift* Won class B, and *Ariel* was second in Class A. Photo: Fran Grenon

Foreword

Writer-sailor Mark J. Gabrielson's new book is a fine, often surprising sea story of men and women who share a distinctively contrarian understanding of what sailing really should be—an adventure by amateur sailors in normal cruising boats making their damp, exciting way across rough seas to a beautiful, beckoning, remote destination.

Anybody looking for a true challenge should race a sailboat out of sight of land, many hundreds of miles across the rough Gulf Stream to beautiful, hospitable Bermuda. Once you've tied up to "the Onion Patch," you can pat yourself on the back and announce, "I'm a deep-water sailor." The 645-mile Marion Bermuda Race is one of very few internationally recognized Category 1 ocean races, defined as "races of long distance and well offshore where boats must be completely self-sufficient." A Category 1 boat must be seaworthy and well prepared, and her crew must be skilled and brave.

Putting all this together requires vision and leadership —and not just on the part of the sailors. The race organizers who created the Marion-Bermuda Race introduced a new approach to ocean racing. Historically, ocean racing boats were designed and built to race, and their crews often included professional sailors. The Marion-Bermuda Race took a different path when two sailors (an American and a Bermudian) founded it in 1977, with 104 boats on the starting line. They laid down two rules that broke from the usual ocean race. (1) The entries must be normal cruising boats and; (2) The crews must be amateurs (or as sailors say, Corinthians).

The new race immediately struck a chord. Although *Yachting* magazine publisher Bob Bavier had won an America's Cup and sailed at the very top level with and against professionals, he liked the founders' aim to "get ocean racing back in the reach of the common man."

As Gabrielson tells the story of the 20 Marion Bermuda Races to date, all the elements of a good sea story appear. "Whether forged through a rescue at sea, being thrashed by big seas and heavy wind offshore, or even collectively suffering through a mind-numbing and interminable calm, sailors who race from Marion to Bermuda, and who do so understanding that it's a race to be won as a Corinthian, will remain life-long friends."

That's one very valuable sign of success.

John Rousmaniere, ocean sailor and author of The Annapolis Book of Seamanship, Fastnet, Force 10, A Berth to Bermuda, *and other sailing books.*

The dock at the RHADC is a lively place as yachts arrive and everyone dresses ship. Photo: Fran Grenon

Contents

Karina in calmer conditions than the 1979 race. Photo: Nancy Braitmayer

Introduction

The night of Sunday, June 24, 1979 was not the best for Jack Braitmayer and his crew of five close friends. They were racing Braitmayer's semi-custom Alden 42 ketch *Karina* in their first Marion-Bermuda Race, a 645-mile sprint offshore from New England to Bermuda.[1] Braitmayer is a Corinthian sailor; he sails his own yacht with an all-amateur crew whenever he competes. He spent his boyhood on the water, learning the basics of competitive sailing from his father in Sippican Harbor and Buzzards Bay off Marion, MA. He had cruised and raced his entire life in family-owned boats. But on that June night in 1979, when Jack was 52, he wasn't sure *Karina* would even get to Bermuda. His logbook shows that at 0100 the wind was building. The anemometer showed 15-20 knots sustained at that point. Navigator Mike Hayden was calling the course to steer. Except for a compass and a bulky radio direction finder (RDF), Hayden's celestial observations were the only navigational information his skipper was getting. And that wasn't very accurate. It was no fault of Mike's. Ever since 0230 the night before, *Karina* had been enveloped in thick fog and the sky was completely obscured. Jack did have a thermometer aboard, an essential piece of equipment for sailors traversing the Gulf Stream. A spike in water temperature is a clear indicator a vessel has entered the Stream. But *Karina* didn't have the convenient digitals wired to hull sensors used today. Instead, Braitmayer used a thermometer dipped in a bucket of seawater hoisted aboard for the purpose. The latest measurement showed that the ocean water temperature was beginning to rise. This was bad. Simultaneously rising wind speed and temperature are a combination Bermuda-bound sailors don't like to see. It means heavy wind could combine with current, unpredictable squalls, and often tumultuous heavy seas in the Gulf Stream for rough conditions. If the wind blew strong counter to the current, seas could build to a frightening size.

By 0600 *Karina* was straining under sustained winds of 35 knots, with gusts up to 40. Jack and his friends had furled the mizzen and genoa, reefed the main, and hanked on a working jib. At 1100, the water temperature spiked to 77 degrees; *Karina* was in the Stream. Moments later, an enormous blast of wind and wave hit. *Karina* was knocked down on her beam ends by a powerful and sudden Gulf Stream squall. Spreaders scraped the tops of waves. The RDF came loose and crashed across the now vertical cabin sole. Amazingly, the beast still functioned when it was called on later in the race as *Karina* approached Bermuda.

Jack learned how to sail and race the way most Corinthian sailors do. They start young, fall in love with the camaraderie, competition, and aesthetics of the sport, and try to become better at it every time they leave the dock. Jack had served in the Air Force during the Korean War, and still had sailing on his mind. While stationed in Okinawa, Sergeant Braitmayer chose "Weather Observer" duty to better develop his meteorological skills in the hopes that it might improve his seamanship. When he returned to civilian life, he built a specialty chemicals business in northern New Jersey, but even then, lived on the Connecticut coast so he could get out onto the salt water. When he sold that business, he moved back to Marion and had his first *Karina* built by the Paul Luke yard in East Boothbay, Maine.

He had *Karina* built with the Marion-Bermuda Race in mind. He was attracted to the fact that it was a Corinthian

The 2015 Marion-Bermuda Race gets underway in Buzzards Bay. The race remains one of the premier Corinthian ocean races. Photo: Fran Grenon

ocean race; a race in which a skipper and his own boat are tested against others and their own boats. It was a contest that brought out not only the best ocean racing, but best preparation, management, provisioning, and selection of unpaid crew; all voluntary, and all the complete responsibility of the owner/skipper of the competing yachts.

Jack wanted to win the Marion-Bermuda Race so badly that he had four *Karinas* built over the seven times he raced to Bermuda. He said in an interview: "I kept building new boats hoping this would be the one to win!"

After the Sunday knockdown in the Gulf Stream, the engine wouldn't start. *Karina* also didn't have a generator. They had no means of recharging system batteries. Bilge pumps and running lights became top priorities. No unessential electric power was to be used. Heavy winds raged. Crewman Peter Demerest cracked a rib on a bulkhead corner when he has thrown across the cabin while pulling on his foulies. He would remain in pain, and very limited in what he could do, all the way to Bermuda.

At noon the next day, the log showed winds still sustained at 30-40 knots. *Karina* and her crew were exhausted, but they finally cleared the Stream. Seas moderated to a more reasonable 6 feet.

Tuesday, June 26 dawned clear and *Karina* romped towards Bermuda at 7 knots under the mizzen, double-reefed main, and working jib in a strong nor'easter from astern. The worst was over. The crew could relax and recover. In the darkness at 0332 on Wednesday June 26, *Karina* crossed the finish line off St. David's head on the eastern end of Bermuda, her running lights dim from a lack of amperage in the battery bank. Jack sailed a few easy reaches until nautical sunrise brightened the eastern sky. Fortunately for the engine-less *Karina*, there was a gentle easterly blowing that morning so Braitmayer and his crew of Hayden, Demerest, Dick and David Webb, and Rick Wilson sailed the boat through the narrow reef entrance off St. George's, then down the length of Bermuda's northern shore

Jack Braitmayer (third from right) and his *Karina* crew celebrate a class win in 1993. Photo: Jack Braitmayer.

and through the pin-hole entrance to Hamilton Harbor, one of the world's most protected bodies of salt water. In the bright morning light, these tired sailors from Marion sailed Jack's 42-foot Alden right up to the wharf in front of the elegant Princess Hotel. Their only regret was that at that time of day, there wasn't anybody around to see them make their turn into the wind for a perfect wharf landing under sail. Braitmayer called it an "eggshell" landing; so gentle nothing was broken. Their 1979 race was over.

The Principles of the Marion-Bermuda Race

The Marion-Bermuda Race is one of the premier long distance ocean races in the North Atlantic. This biennial race, held on odd-numbered years, starts near the head of Buzzards Bay off the historic town of Marion, MA and finishes 645 nautical miles away off St. David's Head on the eastern end of Bermuda. The race is overseen by a board of Trustees, organized and operated by an organizing committee of Bermudian and American volunteers, and is sponsored by the Beverly Yacht Club in Marion, the Royal Hamilton Amateur Dinghy Club in Bermuda, and the Blue Water Sailing Club with members in New England and all along the eastern seaboard.

The Marion-Bermuda Race is unique. It was originally designed for and continues to embody purely Corinthian yacht racing. Active paid professionals are excluded, and organizers carefully vet any sailors with professional sailing backgrounds to ensure that they will compete in the race with a Corinthian spirit.

The word "Corinthian" was invented by the ancient Greeks. Put simply, to be Corinthian was to be of Corinth, a flourishing port city to the west of, and in competition with, Athens. Corinth was home to one of the four major athletic festivals of the ancient Greeks.[2] These "Isthmian" games, as they were called, rivaled the Olympic games in size and splendor in ancient Greece. Like the original Olympic games, all the athletes were amateur (nearly all aristocrats as well), and the idea of sportsmanship, and competing for the sake of honor instead of prizes or compensation, was considered the highest ideal.

Yachting historian John Rousmaniere has written about the origins of Corinthian yacht racing, and how the idea was somewhat radical when it reemerged in the more modern world:

The image of a "Corinthian" as a buttoned-up, blue-blazered, stiff-necked amateur yachtsman is relatively new. The word originated with the citizens of the ancient port of Corinth who were famous both as fine sailors and as exuberant risk-takers in numerous activities, legal and otherwise. "It was a place of proverbial wickedness, energy, riches, noise," A.N. Wilson says of first-century Corinth. Evidence of the rebellious nature of the Corinthians can be found in the New Testament

in St. Paul's chiding letters to the city's early Christians. Centuries later, Shakespeare had wild young prince Hal describe himself as "a Corinthian, a lad of mettle, a good boy." So, when young American and British amateur racing sailors 150 years or so ago called themselves and their yacht clubs "Corinthian," they were identifying their efforts as a revolution. The skill and courage required for a volunteer sailor to prepare, command, and crew a big, fragile racing sailboat in a very professional (and very rough) game were noteworthy. So too was the love of risk that lay behind it—a daring not always found among professionals and their wealthy patrons.[3]

In the modern world, the Corinthian sporting ethic was cultivated by the British (and Bermudians), followed by the Americans, and reached its apogee in the late nineteenth century. A number of Corinthian yacht clubs were formed at that time, largely in reaction to the professionalization of competitive sailing. The historian of one of those clubs wrote: "The founders … adopted a threefold statement of purpose: Becoming proficient in navigation; [maintaining] the personal management, control and handling of their yachts; [and excelling in] all matters pertaining in seamanship."[4] Competence in navigation, personal control of their own yachts, and excellence in seamanship; this book will show that these three tenets were, and remain, the essence of the Marion-Bermuda Race.

James Barnes and his Little Harbor 60 *Lynley III* at the Class A start of the 2013 race. Photo: Fran Grenon

The 2003 race gets underway in Buzzards Bay. Photo: Fran Grenon

Origins:
"A Race from My House
to Your House"

The Marion-Bermuda Race was conceived of in 1972, developed and refined over the next four years, and first raced in 1977. The 1970s were transitional years in ocean yacht racing. Three things were happening simultaneously: first, materials and electronic technologies were reducing the cost, widening the availability and improving the reliability of production sailing yachts. There were significant advances in communications, navigation, materials and safety technologies. The 1970s was when glass-reinforced plastics, an ideal boat-building material, moved from new to mainstream, and when microelectronics entered the world of recreational marine navigation. More and more people could, and were, buying and equipping sailboats with blue water range. These developments made a race from New England to Bermuda by Corinthian-minded cruising sailors not an entirely irrational idea.

Second, racing rules and rating schemes were becoming more sophisticated and more accurate. Racing associations were forming, and were giving the sport a means to apply the more precise rating systems. This meant that more and more often, regattas could accommodate a wide variety of sailboats in a way that skippers felt that the race was "fair."

And third, ocean racing and its organizers were learning from their mistakes. In the 1970s, the most sought-after yacht designers were those able to produce new boats that performed best under the latest and increasingly refined rating schemes. Paradoxically, these trends produced boats that were fast, but only under certain conditions found on a closed inshore course. Successful sailors took these new specialized boats into ocean races, and often won. The problem with the ocean is that conditions change; sometimes suddenly and dramatically. Specialized boats can encounter weather and sea conditions that are well beyond the design's intended use. The best example of this was the 1979 Fastnet Race off southern England and Ireland, the worst ocean racing catastrophe of all time. That August, just two months after *Karina* and 124 other cruising yachts had completed the 645-nautical mile passage to Hamilton in the second Marion-Bermuda Race, fifteen sailors died in the western approaches to the English Channel. Of the 303 boats in that race, 5 sank, 75 were flipped, and 100 were rolled on their side. John Rousmaniere published his analysis of that race and the yachts racing in it in his best-selling book *Fastnet Force 10*:

> "The Fastnet disaster forced sailors to ask some tough questions about their boats... There had been a generational shift in yacht design during the 1970s. Before then, the typical stock cruiser-racer was narrow, heavy and extremely stable. But then came the intensification of competition and the tweaking of the measurement rule (the International Offshore Rule, or IOR) that was used in racing to provide a standard of comparison...A new breed of racing boat appeared that was little more than a big, lightweight dinghy...the problem was that a typical thirty-five-footer in 1979 was much less stable than a typical boat the same length a decade earlier."[5]

An article in *Sailing World* recalls the 1979 Fastnet disaster. *Sailing World* magazine. June, 2002

The 1979 Fastnet was a watershed in ocean racing. It forced rating associations, designers and skippers to recognize and reassess the tradeoffs between seaworthiness and all-out speed. The international Offshore Racing Council and national sailing associations soon established and enforced rating rules and safety standards. The 1979 Fastnet also led to the establishment of "Safety at Sea" courses and seminars. The Marion-Bermuda Race and the US Naval Academy pioneered the earliest symposia.

Indirectly, the Marion-Bermuda Race would benefit from this renewed emphasis on sea safety. Rating systems were modified to reemphasize important seaworthiness variables like righting moments and stability. Seaworthiness became paramount, and early in the history of Marion-Bermuda the passage to Bermuda became safer for a new yacht built and handled well for the ocean.

The creative origins of the Marion-Bermuda Race lie in the unlikely but fortuitous encounter of two men: William David ("Dave") Kingery and Geoffrey Richard ("Dickie") Bird. In the summer of 1972 Kingery, his wife Trudy, and their teenage son were on the homeward leg of a remarkable family voyage. They arrived in Bermuda having spent a full year sailing from their summer home in Marion, Massachusetts to and from Tahiti aboard their 50' Columbia sloop *Keramos*. Kingery moored *Keramos* at the Royal Hamilton Amateur Dinghy Club (RHADC). The

Dickie Bird and David Kingery together in 1993. The two met in 1972 and through their friendship founded the Marion-Bermuda Race. Photo: *Marion-Bermuda Cruising Yacht Race* book. 1995

RHADC clubhouse and docks preside over the head of lovely Hamilton harbor. Kingery, Bird, and their families met on the dock at the RHADC marina. In recent interviews, Trudy Kingery said that Dickie Bird was one of the most gregarious people she and David had ever encountered. They liked him immediately.

In an illuminating personal memo to his own files titled "The History of the Bermuda Cruising Yacht Race" written shortly before he died in 2011, Bird took the time to document his early encounters with Dave and Trudy[6]. By the time he wrote the memo the race was in its fourth decade and had been run seventeen times. By then he knew that he and Kingery had created something important. He wrote:

"In 1972, Professor David Kingery, who held the Chair of Ceramics at the Massachusetts Institute of Technology, was awarded a sabbatical year during which time he was able to carry out some projects

of occupation which he had always wished to do but had no time.

He decided to sail from the USA East Coast to Tahiti and back. He purchased a fifty foot Colombia (*sic*) yacht and fitted it out for an ocean passage.

He was accompanied by his wife and teenage son who, owing to the length of the voyage, had to be educated during the trip and David and his wife Trudy carried out the school syllabus while at sea.

On his return trip from the Pacific Ocean heading back to Marion, he stopped in Bermuda as he had rented his house in Marion and the period of the tenancy had not yet expired.

He therefore decided to stay in Bermuda for some three or four weeks and moored his yacht at the RHADC and quickly made a number of close friends at that establishment.

My yacht the *Water Gypsy* was moored opposite *Keramos* on the Dinghy Club camber and we quickly became good friends… David and I sometimes discussed at length organizing a cruising yacht race from Marion to Bermuda."

Kingery sailed to Bermuda single-handed in 1975 to fulfill a qualification requirement for the OSTAR (Original Solo Transatlantic Race) race from Plymouth, England to Newport, Rhode Island, which he planned to enter the following June. It was a difficult passage for Kingery, but not for the expected reasons. Bird wrote:

"I further met David in 1975 when he raced single handedly from the USA to Bermuda. At that time, he had ambitions to sail the Atlantic single handed but on setting his foot on Bermuda, he said he had given up the idea because when sailing single handed there was nobody with whom to talk."

On January 3, 1976 Dickie and his then-wife Jan joined the Kingerys aboard *Keramos* in Antigua, and the couples enjoyed a leisurely cruise through what Bird referred to as the "West Indies" touching at St. Bartholomew, Isle, Fourche, St. Kitts, Montserrat and elsewhere. They returned to Antigua, and the Birds helped the Kingerys sail *Keramos* back north to Bermuda. Bird remembered that trip for how the two founders outlined the general principles of the original race:

"Early in this cruise David and I discussed at length and noted many details that were still outstanding in the race organization. Sitting every night at the cockpit of *Keramos*, and with the yellow pad on his knees, we formulated the general conditions that we [thought] could be attractive and fairly simple compared to most ocean races. The salient matters as I recall were that:

> Boats would be limited in size from Thirty to Fifty Feet overall
> Offshore Racing Council category 3 minimum equipment and safety standards
> No spinnakers allowed, and limited sail inventory
> No radio connections
> No professional sailors, and only Astro navigation and many other requirements
> Special categories to include short-handed and family crews etc."

With a twinkle in her eye, Trudy Kingery said in one of our interviews that David put the fifty-foot upper limit in because "He didn't want any entries bigger than *Keramos*." This may or may not be apocryphal, and the length limit in the 1977 race became 60 feet anyway, but Kingery and Bird clearly were designing a new race they would want

to sail in; a race that reflected their ideals and interests[7]. It was to be a race with "no professional sailors," a true Corinthian event, with limited sail inventory, and a bias against the newer radio navigation methods then becoming available to recreational sailors. It also would be a race that they hoped could attract adventuresome family and short-handed crews. At the time, these were relatively unique ideas in blue water racing.

Several witnesses have reported that Bird and Kingery said that they wanted to run a race "from my house to your house." So much is packed into that short phrase. In an interview in 1995 published in Bermuda's *Royal Gazette*, Bird said:

"We know all the people up here [in Marion] … They've all become very close friends for me. It's been 20 years now and it's always a great delight to come up here. I mean there aren't even any hotels here so when people come up everybody stays in everybody's houses. It really is a bit like old home week and then they come to Bermuda and we do the same thing for them."

Of course, Kingery intended the race to run from Marion, Massachusetts to the Bird's home of Hamilton, Bermuda. But the notion of his "house" connotes his interest in attracting more amateurs and families to meaningful competitive ocean racing. Kingery could have said from "my country to your country," or from "my club to your club," but he didn't. Kingery and Bird were reaching for something different.

With their plan in hand, the two men approached their respective clubs. Kingery met with the Bridge officers of the Blue Water Sailing Club, a New England-centered sailing club without a clubhouse, analogous to the older, and far larger, Cruising Club of America. Kingery chaired the Blue

Water Sailing Club Offshore Committee at the time and was responsible for engaging the membership in offshore adventures. He received the enthusiastic support of Commodore Leo Fallon, who on September 10, 1975 wrote a letter proposing to Commodore Coles R. Diel of the RHADC that the two clubs co-sponsor Kingery and Bird's race. A letter from Diel back to Fallon dated September 23, 1975 said:

> "…I am happy to inform you that our Committee of Management has already agreed that the Royal Hamilton Amateur Dinghy Club should sponsor the race you have mentioned in your letter."

Dickie Bird had paved the way. The letter from Diel goes on to say:

> "Our committee will be pleased to work with David Kingery as you suggest…and endorse all of the comments that you have made about the race being a cruising race."

Kingery also was a member of the Beverly Yacht Club, one of the great and established racing clubs on Buzzards Bay. With an elegant but unpretentious clubhouse and wharf on Sippican Harbor in Marion, BYC was the perfect place to base the pre-race and starting line operations for the new event.

On October 8, 1975, Kingery sent another letter to Commodore Diel reinforcing the basic ideas of the race, including limiting sails (for example, no spinnakers allowed), and provisions he thought would "encourage conservative seamanship." In this letter he also announced that he and the Blue Water Sailing Club would be organizing a cruising yacht race that would run from Boston to St. John, New Brunswick in the summer of 1976 and solic-

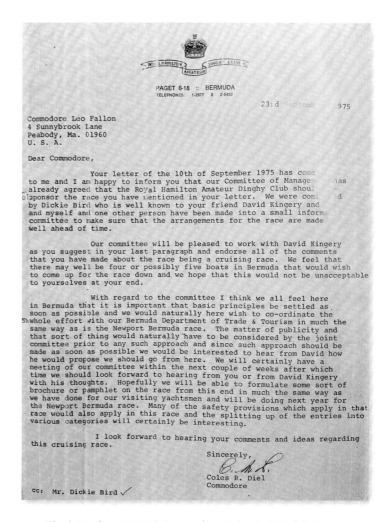

The letter from RHADC Commodore Coles R. Diel dated 23 September, 1975 informing Blue Water Sailing Club Commodore Leo Fallon that through Dickie Bird's efforts, and at David Kingery's initiative, the RHADC accepted the opportunity to co-sponsor the first Marion-Bermuda Race. Photo: RHADC Archives

ited the RHADC committee's comments on a draft race announcement. Kingery was thinking that this opportunity to comment could smoke out any potential disagreements over principles that would apply to the inaugural Marion-Bermuda Race, which indeed it did.

The test race was titled the "Blue Water Bicentennial

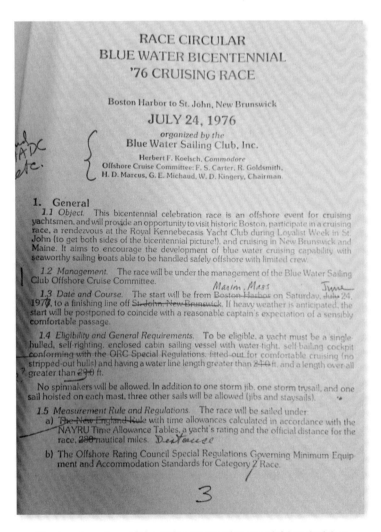

The hand markup of the "Blue Water Bicentennial '76 Cruising Race" Race Circular. David Kingery used the 1976 race to the Royal Kennebecasis Yacht Club in St. John, Nova Scotia to test the rules and regulations of a new ocean race. The 1976 Race Circular became the substrate for the 1977 Marion-Bermuda Race circular. Photo: by the Author. RHADC Archives

'76 Cruising Race" in honor of the nation's two hundredth anniversary. Dickie Bird and the RHADC committee took a pen to that '76 "Race Circular". With surprisingly few edits, their markup became, by today's NOR standards, the amazingly simple four-page "Race Circular, Blue Water Cruising Race, Marion-Bermuda June 25, 1977."

With two official sponsoring clubs, and the Beverly Yacht Club ready to coordinate registration, starting arrangements, and provide a venue for the principle social events in Marion, Kingery and Bird had their race.

Excitement in the Press

Publicity got underway in earnest in the summer of 1976. *SAIL* and *Cruising World* carried stories describing this new and different yacht race from Marion to Bermuda planned for the summer of 1977. Bob Bavier at *Yachting* took notice as well. Bavier and *Yachting* were at the top of the sport's establishment at the time, his blessing was very influential.[8] He wrote in the October 1976 issue that the new race:

"… is intended to get ocean racing back in the reach of the common man…As David Kingery, chairman of the event, pointed out, they felt that it's not so much the rating rule which discourages many owners of cruising auxiliaries from competing as it is the fact that the boats competing in the major races have no restrictions as to sail inventory, numbers in crew, or type of accommodations."[9]

When he summed up the results of the first race in the October, 1977 issue of *Yachting*, Tony Gibbs wrote:

"Almost from the moment of its announcement ("From the Cockpit" by Bob Bavier, October, 1976) the first Blue Water Cruising Race was a box-office smash."

Bermuda's *Royal Gazette* interviewed Dickie Bird and other members of the RHADC committee. The *Gazette* said that the race:

"…will become an important new offshore event for yachtsmen… The importance of this event, as the name implies, is that it will offer the opportunity for the cruising yachtsman to compete in offshore racing; in fact, it is expected that 'cruising families' will participate… It is hoped that this cruising race will counteract the trend of recent years to races between ever more highly specialized racing machines with a racing life of only two or three years." [10]

Kingery and Bird were up against some stiff event competition. They had to keep the far older and larger Newport Bermuda Race in mind as they designed and scheduled the race. Since 1906, the "Bermuda Race" had been sailed regularly from some point in or near Long Island Sound to Bermuda, almost always biennially, and usually on even-numbered years. The race attracted very large fleets of racers, and although the Newport Bermuda Race permits professional sailors to compete in separate classes, most were competitors, and still are, Corinthian sailors. [11]

On odd-numbered years, there already were two sailing races planned from New England to Bermuda: the Bermuda One-Two, also in its inaugural year running from Newport to St. George's, and the Multihull Bermuda Race, sailed occasionally from new London to Bermuda since 1967. Furthermore, the Annapolis-Newport Race also was sailed on odd-numbered years, typically early in June, and the Marion-Bermuda Race organizers may have understood that by scheduling the start later in the month, they might have a "feeder" race opportunity for their new event. So they decided to start the race on Saturday, June 25, 1977.

SAIL assessed the crowded 1977 Bermuda race calendar: "Of the three…races, the one from Marion is potentially the most significant. Its concept seems to appeal to a lot

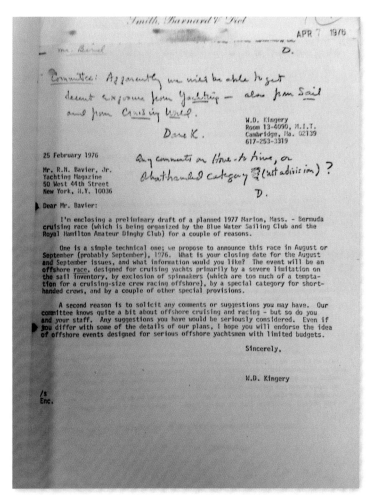

David Kingery wrote letters like this one to Bob Bavier of *Yachting* announcing the 1977 Marion-Bermuda Race, and asking for input on race rules. Bavier and others responded with enthusiasm. Photo: by the Author. RHADC Archives

of people." [12] Kingery and Bird, and their supporters, had discovered a gap in competitive sailing. Given the extraordinary publicity and turnout for the first race, the sailing press and the racing community agreed.

Geoffrey R. "Dickie" Bird

In a recent interview, Rhonda Fantasia said that Dickie Bird was a "gorgeous man." She went on to elaborate. He was "gorgeous" in both appearance and demeanor. She said, "whatever Dave Kingery lacked in personality, Dickie Bird had, and more." He had a "presence." Personalities such as this can do things, and Dickie Bird was certainly a doer.

Dickie was born in 1922 in Lowenstoft, Sussex, a port town on the eastern coast of England. His family owned and operated the White Hart Hotel and Restaurant. As a tavern kid, Dickie developed his aptitude for making new acquaintances feel instantly

This pastel of the White Hart Hotel in Lowenstoft hangs in Jean Bird's home in Bermuda. Photo: by the Author

comfortable. He also learned the nuts and bolts of the hotel trade that would serve him well later in his Bermuda career.

In late 1939, barely aged 18, Dickie enlisted in the Royal Navy's Fleet Air Arm. Including his training, he flew seven types of aircraft in World War II, distinguishing himself as both a pilot and air gunnery officer. Drawings of his seven airplanes hang on the study wall in his widow Jean Bird's house in Bermuda. Jean told me that Dickie was proud he flew for the Navy and not the Royal Air Force. Dickie and his fellow RN pilots would refer to the RAF pilots as the "Brylcream Boys" for all the attention they received.

When the European war ended in May of 1945, Dickie Bird had completed a career in naval aviation that included carrier landings, a ditch at sea, and commendations for service

Drawings of the seven-different aircraft Dickie Bird flew in WWII hang in Jean Bird's home in Bermuda. Photo: by the Author

R. Geoffrey "Dickie" Bird, the gregarious Bermudian and former Fleet Air Arm pilot from Lowenstoft, Sussex, UK. Photo: RHADC Archives

including the Russian Convoy Medal, Malta Defence Medal, Defence Medal, the General Service Medal, the Atlantic Star, the Italy Star and the 1939-1945 star. [13]

Dickie Bird moved from post-war England to Bermuda in 1948 to "carry out the $300,000 refurbishment of the Princess Hotel." He went on in a public service career as Hamilton's first City Engineer from 1950-1963 and oversaw the construction of Hamilton's landmark City Hall. But perhaps he is best known for commissioning the small, hexagonal roofed shelter for traffic police in the

Dickie Bird poses proudly
in front of the RHADC.
Photo: RHADC Archives

intersection of Front and Queen Streets in Hamilton. Jean said his motives were simple—give the poor police officer at that busy intersection some protection from the sun and weather. Tourists and locals know it as the "Birdcage," although many think it's named after its design, not its designer. Dickie Bird also is credited with (some say blamed for) Bermuda's first condominiums, a complex called Roxdene on Pitt's Bay Road in Pembroke.

His many business interests gave way to leadership service at the RHADC, the Royal Naval Officers Association, the Mariners Club and the Bermuda Sailors Home. According to his obituary, and as evidenced by the elegantly-framed certificates hanging in Jean's home, he was "twice recognized on the Queen's Honours list for services to maritime affairs in Bermuda." A uniformed Dickie Bird usually marched in Hamilton's Remembrance Day parade on Front Street each November.

Jean related that Dickie was a "raconteur, a bibliophile, an accomplished improvisational speaker, and a lover of limericks." He loved to sing. He was an enthusiastic member of the barbershop group "Grate Sounders." Jean said that his favorite song was "Lavender Cowboy," a not-so-politically correct Burl Ives song about a cowboy with only two chest hairs. But Dickie probably didn't care—he liked the way it sounded, and so he sang it.

Dickie Bird died in the spring of 2011, and one of his lasting legacies is the Marion-Bermuda Race.

27

W. David Kingery

What Dickie Bird had in personality and color, Dave Kingery had in creative imagination and implementation skills. As sports entrepreneurs, the two men may have been close to an ideal partnership.

William David Kingery was born in 1927 in White Plains, NY near Long Island Sound [14]. He was a brilliant student. He graduated from MIT in 1948 and after only two more years of study, was awarded a PhD in ceramics in 1950. He immediately joined the faculty at MIT where he ascended the academic ranks to eventually head the Department of Ceramics in the 1970s.

It's important to know that Kingery's "ceramics" was not what most of us think of when we hear the word. His field was not pottery wheels and kilns. Kingery's ceramics was at the leading edge of advanced materials sciences. *The New York Times* noted in his July, 2000 obituary that:

"Dr. Kingery's work on advanced materials technology in ceramics...was vastly different from the hands-on methods that produced bricks, china, pottery and glass from natural materials through the ages. He built upon recent advances in high polymers, solid-state physics and crystallography to bring ceramics into the era of aerospace electronics and engineering."

David Kingery was a world-renowned scientist and leader in his discipline. He wrote the leading text in the field, published more than 200 scientific papers, and was a Fellow of the American Academy of Arts and Sciences as well as the American Association for the Advancement of Science. Late in his career the awards poured in. In 1998 he was awarded the first "W. David Kingery Award" of the American

MIT Professor and Marion-Bermuda Race co-founder David Kingery. Photo: *Cruising World*. November, 1977. 101

Ceramics Society. In 1999 he was awarded the Kyoto Prize in Materials Sciences and Engineering, the Nobel Prize of his field. When MIT renovated and then reopened their "MIT Glass Lab" in 2015, they renamed it the "W. David Kingery Ceramics and Glass Laboratory." Kingery founded Lexington Labs, a company hired by the US government to create "clear crystals," an extraordinarily difficult technical challenge.

His friend Joe Fantasia, who became David's right-hand man in the early years of Marion-Bermuda race planning and implementation and went on to the chair the race, described David as a big guy and a good sailor. "If something broke, he could fix it" said Fantasia. Kingery loved competitive sailboat racing, in boats both large and small. He joined the venerable Beverly Yacht Club in Marion. He was a pretty good sailor of International 110s, a narrow 24' double-ended

ASTEROID (left) with Keramos (centre), owned by race founder David Kingery, also rac year, and Bandit at the start of the 1983 event.

Dave Kingery's Columbia 50 *Keramos* at the start of the 1983 Marion-Bermuda Race. Photo: *The Royal Gazette*

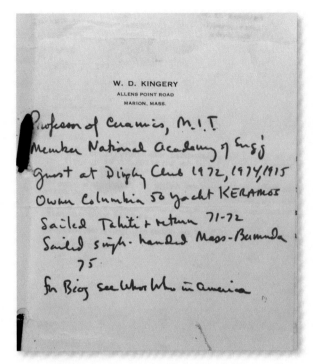

W. D. KINGERY
ALLENS POINT ROAD
MARION, MASS.

Professor of Ceramics, M.I.T
Member National Academy of Engg
Guest at Dinghy Club 1972, 1974/1975
Owner Columbia 50 yacht KERAMOS
Sailed Tahiti + return 71-72
Sailed single-handed Mass-Bermuda
75.
For Biog see Who Who in America

David Kingery's "Application" for membership to the
RHADC. Undated. Photo: RHADC Archives

The "FOUNDERS" of
Marion - Bermuda Cruising Yacht Race

W. David Kingery   G. R. "Dickie" Bird
1926 - 2000   1922 - 2011

This plaque memorializing Dickie Bird and David Kingery
as co-founders of the Marion-Bermuda Race hangs
in the front foyer of the RHADC in Bermuda.
An identical plaque hangs in the main lounge of the
Beverly Yacht Club in Marion, MA. Photo: by the Author

racing sloop common in Buzzards Bay.

He based his Columbia 50 *Keramos* in Marion where
he owned a summer home. He named the boat after the
ancient Greek city of Keramos which lay on the north coast
of the Ceramic Gulf, an indentation of the Aegean Sea into
the south west coast of present day Turkey. Craftsmen of
Keramos produced the world's earliest ceramics.

David also belonged to the Blue Water Sailing Club, a
New England-centered virtual yacht club founded in 1959
and dedicated to promoting open ocean sailing and cruising.
In 1971 he took a sabbatical from MIT, rented out his home
on Allen's Point Rd. in Marion, and he and his wife Trudy and
their son took off in *Keramos* for Tahiti.

On their way back in June, 1972 they stopped in
Bermuda, running ahead of schedule, and there they were
adopted by the Birds and the RHADC.

In 1988 Kingery accepted a faculty position at the
University of Arizona, another top department in his field.
Curious as to why an east coast blue water sailor would
move to Arizona, I was told by Trudy Kingery that he had
reached an "inflection point" in his life and needed a change.
Arizona also attracted him due to an interest in Native
American ceramics, horses and aviation. Joe Fantasia
related how Kingery had an eventful career as a private
pilot, including having to make a forced landing in his light
plane in the desert. He died in 2000, but by that point his
direct involvement in the Marion-Bermuda race largely had
ended. However, in commemoration of his contributions, the
Marion-Bermuda Race Trustees commissioned two identical
bronze plaques. Bird and Kingery now greet all visitors to
both the RHADC and Beverly Yacht Club in the clubs' front
foyers. They show the two founders grinning at one another.

Class B powering up to cross the line at the start of the 2005 Marino-Bermuda Race. Photo: Fran Grenon

CHAPTER 2

An Instant Success in 1977

"The race's co-sponsors…had been anticipating an entry list running between 30 and 50 yachts. When the applicants reached 125 with no end in sight, the organizers wisely pulled the string…"

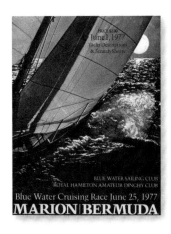

So reported *Yachting* in the September, 1977 issue. Of the 125 applicants, organizers permitted 110 yachts to enter the first Marion-Bermuda race. Of these, 104 crossed the starting line and shaped a course for Bermuda in a fresh southwesterly. Ironically, one of the six boats that couldn't cross the line was Dickie Bird's *Water Gypsy*.

He and his crew had departed Hamilton two weeks prior and sailed to Marion where they would be welcomed into local homes as guests. This was, and remains, a uniqueness of the Marion-Bermuda Race. Marion is a small and picturesque New England village, completely engaged with the sea throughout its history. However, there are no hotels in Marion. Bird, the other five Bermuda-registered competitors, and the organizers from the RHADC were given accommodations in Marion homes, some among the most magnificent waterfront houses on the eastern seaboard. When the American Marion-Bermuda organizers, Trustees, and sponsoring club officers visit Bermuda, they too are accommodated in RHADC homes. This welcoming reciprocity results in unusually strong and lasting friendships among race organizers and competitors.

Keramos at the start of the 1977 Marion-Bermuda Race. Photo: Trudy Kingery

Friendship only goes so far, however. In the starting box, teeth are bared and maneuvering is aggressive, perhaps especially among Corinthian sailors. They are trying to squeeze out an advantage of a few feet prior to a 645 nautical mile passage. Bird was maneuvering his 34-foot Swedish-built Singoalla sloop *Water Gypsy* into position in close quarters. *Yachting* magazine reported what happened next:

"There were a number of close calls [at the start], but only one collision, when … *Salty Dawg*, on port tack, plowed into the stern of a Bermuda boat, Geoffrey Bird's *Water Gypsy*, causing her to lose her backstay and drop out." [15]

Dickie Bird never sailed in a Marion-Bermuda Race again. He remained active on both ends of the race, however. In short order he was elected Rear Commodore of the RHADC, ascended the ranks, and was Commodore in 1990-1991. Each race year he would visit Marion for planning meetings and pre-race receptions, always adding to his ever-widening circle of friends there. After the finish, he would welcome them all to Bermuda and the RHADC.

The 104 yachts that did cross the starting line sailed out of Buzzards Bay on a gentle breeze. Near the front in Class A was *Keramos* skippered by Dave Kingery with former BWSC Commodore Leo Fallon in his crew. The fleet was remarkably diverse. There were 55 sloops, 27 yawls, 18 ketches, 9 cutters and one schooner. Six yachts hailed from Bermuda and five from the US Naval Academy (three of which had competed in the Annapolis-Newport Race the week prior). Two yachts hailed from Canada, and one was registered in the British Virgin Islands. The smallest yacht was the 29' 10" Irwin sloop *Bacchus* sailed by K.A. Tedeschi of Hanover, MA. The largest was the 59' 8" Hood ketch *Tioga* under the command of B. P. Noyes, and sailed largely by the Noyes family of Marblehead, MA.

The average overall length was 39' 9".

The organizers had settled on the New England Yacht Rating Rule to handicap the diverse fleet. The NEYRR was one of several predecessors to the PHRF rating system common in cruising yacht racing today. According to *SAIL*, "…the rule works out so that boats built to the International Offshore Rule are rated 10 to 25 percent higher than they would be under IOR." [16] The organizers further applied an adjustment to each boat's New England Rating designed to favor cruising yachts with smaller sail plans. The Marion-Bermuda Race organizers chose a rating system and adjustments that deliberately deemphasized several design elements in the so-called "IOR" boats, boats that had been disproportionally overwhelmed by the extraordinary conditions of the 1979 Fastnet race.

Kingery and the Race Committee organized the fleet into 7 classes. The scratch boat was the 55' 3" custom yawl *Rob Roy* skippered and navigated by K.D. Pittkin of Ft. Lauderdale, FL entered in Class A. The "best" rating went to *Bacchus* in Class E, which would end up having a very eventful race, but for unexpected reasons.

Only 12 of the 110 entries chose to accept a 5% rating penalty, which, according to the Race Circular, would allow them to use electronic navigation equipment at any time. The rest accepted the limitation that LORAN and similar equipment could only be used within the "20 fathom depth contour of the departure coast, and again when estimated to be within 50 miles of Bermuda," and were navigated celestially while at sea. All 110 boats had aboard a person "skilled in and equipped for celestial navigation." [17]

By race rules, none of the boats carried spinnakers. Kingery, Bird and their respective sponsoring clubs had decided that most cruising sailors and their crews should not be fooling around with spinnakers while at sea. It was a safety consideration and typical of their focus on creating a fun and safe race. They also placed limits on other sail

The only known published-photo of the heavily-decorated Tartan 41D *Silkie* sailed by Herb Marcus. *Silkie* and Marcus won the 1977 race overall and on elapsed time, a feat matched only three other times in Marion-Bermuda history. Photo: *The Royal Gazette*

inventories, particularly headsails, hoping to eliminate the sail "arms race" that often stresses budgets in offshore racing.

The fleet sailed out of Buzzards Bay and into the darkness of the first night. By morning, almost all the boats were out of sight of one another. This is an interesting phenomenon in long distance ocean racing. Line of sight limitations due to haze and the Earth's curvature dictates that within 24 hours a boat sailing in the Marion-Bermuda Race will find itself largely alone at sea. Although he didn't know it at the time, Herb Marcus aboard his Tartan 41 sloop *Silkie* were moving well; better than most, in fact. He and his two crewmates (both members of the Elkins family) were sailing fast, short-handed and celestially. While most of the fleet languished in a wind hole sitting right on the Gulf Stream, Marcus and *Silkie* found wind. Marcus said: "We rode a northwesterly right through to the Bermuda side of the Gulf Stream…Our greatest speed, 10 knots, was through the stream." [18] As *Silkie* barreled towards Bermuda, some of his competitors had the time to take a swim as their boats sat still in the water. Mostly because of the calm, 16 boats dropped out of the race and motored to Bermuda.

Meanwhile *Bacchus* encountered a strange situation. According to *SAIL*:

"…one of the smallest boats in the race, an Irwin 30 named *Bacchus*, received special recognition for going to the aid of a boat in distress. *Bacchus* was two days out and about 100 miles south of Nantucket when at 6:30 AM her crew spotted a 25-foot ketch flashing a strobe light and firing flares. They took down their sails and motored over to investigate. As they approached, the boat's lone occupant jumped into the water and began swimming the 50 yards between the two boats. When he reached *Bacchus*, they pulled him aboard.

The Briand 76 *Lilla* owned by Simon De Pietro is one of only four boats to win both elapsed and corrected time honors in the Marion-Bermuda Race. She is shown here at the heavy weather start of the 2011 race. Photo: Fran Grenon

An Instant Success in 1977

Herb Marcus (dark shirt) and his family crew at the end of the 1979 race. Herb and his Tartan 41 sloop *Silkie* remain the most-decorated skipper-boat pair in Marion-Bermuda Race history. Photo: *Bermuda Sun*

check the log. She was the *Margaret D*, a competitor in the singlehanded race and nine days out of Newport. The skipper…had turned back after six days without sighting Bermuda. *Bacchus* stood by for almost 13 hours before a Coast Guard cutter picked up [the skipper] and took the *Margaret D* in tow." [19]

The *Bacchus* crew adhered to the tenet that when at sea one sailor must help another in distress. Over the history of the Marion-Bermuda Race, this fact of sea life has been demanded of its competitors a number of times.

Marcus and *Silkie* were overwhelming victors in the 1977 Marion-Bermuda Race. They won both first to finish, and first on corrected time—the dual win is a relatively rare feat in Marion-Bermuda history. They also won first in Class B and first shorthanded yacht. Marcus also won the Navigator's Trophy presented to the navigator of the first yacht across on corrected time (later changed to the navigator of the first celestially-navigated yacht). *Silkie* would also have won the Tartan 41 mini-class trophy, but mini-class trophies aren't awarded to class winners. *Silkie* had already won Class B.

Sam Norad, one of *Bacchus's* crew, said the man seemed to be hallucinating and suffering from extreme exhaustion. 'He was screaming about people on the boat and that he had been to several ports and nobody would let him in.' Norad said.

When they got the man calmed down and asleep Norad went aboard the boat to tidy things up and

Marcus and *Silkie* were a powerful team. They went on to win silver in the next three Marion-Bermuda races. With 10 total trophies, frequent class wins and first shorthanded yacht titles, Herb Marcus and *Silkie* are the most decorated skipper/yacht pair in Marion-Bermuda history.

Corinthian Resolve: The Story of the Marion-Bermuda Race

The Blue Water Sailing Club

The Blue Water Sailing Club is a sailing club without a club-house. It was founded in 1959 by people who enjoyed racing their cruising yachts, but found a shortage of auxiliary day races and organized cruises by yacht clubs in eastern New England.

Their models were the Off Soundings Club, an organization founded in 1933 by sailors primarily based in western Long Island Sound focused on racing, and the Cruising Club of America, another facility-free yacht club specializing in cruises and the occasional ocean race, most prominently the Newport-Bermuda race.

The first meeting of BWSC founders was held in October 1959 at the Boston Yacht Club's Marblehead station.[21] Seventy-nine people turned up shortly after for the second meeting held in December at MIT, including yacht designer, builder and America's Cup campaigner Ted Hood (later elected a life member). The Blue Water Sailing Club was incorporated and Roger W. Kent elected first Commodore. What followed was rapid growth and a burgeoning program of sailing and social events. By 1979, there were 218 memberships (individuals and couples) including such marine industry notables as Ted Hood, naval architect Dieter Empacher, and marine power systems builder Jack Westerbeke.

BWSC has always been a sailor's club, with ownership of a sailing vessel of at least 20' in length a requirement for entry. Although later dropped, a provision in the original membership requirements clearly states that the Blue Water Sailing Club was exclusively for sailors: "Any member purchasing a motorboat or motor sailer (sic) will be automatically dropped from the roles...". Today, a small group of BWSC members own power yachts as their principal club vessel, but all are prior sailboat owners and joined the club as such.

Apart from the Marion-Bermuda Race, all Blue Water Sailing Club's races and regattas have been organized by

The Blue Water Sailing Club organizes cruises in Maine, Long Island Sound, cruises crewed entirely by women, and other events throughout the year. This photo was taken on the 2012 Maine cruise. See www.bluewatersc.org and www.facebook.com/bluewatersc. Photo: Christine Aubin

and on behalf of its members and their guests. The Club originally raced under Off Soundings Club rules, and had a "Measurer" as part of its officer corps. More recently, like most yacht clubs Blue Water Sailing Club races use the PHRF handicap, widely and readily available for cruising yachts. The club has organized races to St. John, NB (1976; the "test" race for the 1977 inaugural Marion-Bermuda Race, and again in 1990), as well as to Campobello island (1988, 1992 and 1998). Recently, the Blue Water Sailing Club has become known for its organized cruises. The club has an annual cruise to Maine, and another to destinations in Nantucket and Long Island Sounds. The club also organizes an annual Women's Cruise on which women cruise their own boats, those of their spouse, or boats they charter for the purpose to develop and sharpen their sea skills.

The Royal Hamilton Amateur Dinghy Club

The RHADC is among the world's older sailing-oriented clubs. Joseph Trimingham and others were determined to form an organization to give some structure to the Bermuda fitted "Dingey" racing then becoming popular on the island. So in 1882, probably in Trimingham's home, the Hamilton "Dingey" Association was formed[20].

The original RHADC held amateurism in sport in high regard, characteristic of the British, and established Bermudians, in the late nineteenth and early twentieth centuries. At the time, the notion of "amateur" overlapped with "Corinthian." in many ways. Both connoted sport for the fun and honor of competition, not the glory and prestige of the prize. Certainly, both rejected pay-to-play, or professionalism in athletics. Many years later, when David Kingery landed on the dock at the RHADC with a purely Corinthian cruising race in mind, he had arrived at the right spot.

The club was conferred royal status one year after its founding by H.R.H. Princess Louise, Queen Victoria's daughter and at the time Marchioness of Lorne.

ABOVE: The west façade of "Mangroville", circa 1890s. The building on Pomander Road in Paget has been transformed by the club and commands a westerly view of Hamilton harbor. The people in the photo are Mary Ingham and her two daughters Marion and Julia. Photo: RHADC Archives

LEFT: The south façade of the mansion "Mangroville" circa 1890s. The house was the home of Mary Ingham (nee Howard Owen) at the time. It was purchased by the RHADC in the early 1960s to serve as the waterside clubhouse. Photo: RHADC Archives

ABOVE: The Royal Hamilton Amateur Dinghy Club photographed from the mast head of a competitor yacht, June 2011.
Photo: Matthew Wall

LEFT: An aerial view of the RHADC clubhouse on Pomander Road before construction of the mole and marina. Circa 1963.
Photo: RHADC Archives

The Princess hotels in Bermuda are named for her. The Marchioness was visiting Bermuda on a winter holiday. It was also then that the club's unique shore-side ensign (rectangular white with the Union Jack in the canton) was warranted by the Admiralty. However, the club's initial royal status would endure for only seven years. In 1890 the UK altered the procedure governing titles and limited conferring that privilege to reigning monarchs only. However, the RHADC recovered its royal status in 1953 by Queen Elizabeth II in anticipation of her visit to Bermuda, and the RHADC, in 1954.

Under the leadership of Commodore H. L. Williams (whose son, H. Allan Williams served as Commodore 2011–2013), the club acquired the "Mangroville" mansion at the head of Hamilton Harbor in Paget in 1964. RHADC then moved its clubhouse from Church St. in Hamilton to this commanding waterfront location. As time passed, the club built out its marina and breakwater.

The mansion has of course been renovated and expanded, and now is a premier yacht club facility with spectacular upper and lower level views to the west. Although awards ceremonies for the Marion-Bermuda race have been held in other locations including the Hamilton Princess Hotel and Royal Naval Dockyards on the western end of the island with its Commissioner's House, the RHADC itself remains a favorite venue for Marion-Bermuda after-race celebrations.

The Marion-Bermuda Race boat *Impulse* in the Gulf Stream photographed by a passing northbound cruising yacht in 1979. Photo: Jay Wurts

Heavy Weather Sailing in 1979 and 1981

"[YACHTING magazine] wanted to signify its support of this contest—already widely imitated—with a major trophy, one that would in its way be as unusual as the race. After considerable thought all around, the Marion-Bermuda founder and race chairman, David Kingery, suggested that he'd long wanted to provide a special seamanship-sportsmanship award, for vessels and/or crews that performed some genuinely noteworthy feat during the race. As a result, YACHTING has donated such a prize, awarded by vote of the Race Committee 'in recognition of outstanding seamanship, sportsmanship, Corinthian spirit or other special contribution to offshore sailing' made during the race. It will be named the Robert N. Bavier Jr. Trophy, in honor of YACHTING'S president and former publisher, who during his long and distinguished sailing career has always advocated high standards of seamanship and sportsmanship in competitive sailing."[22]

What the publishers of *Yachting* couldn't have known when establishing the Bavier trophy is how many candidates for the prize the rough 1979 race would produce.

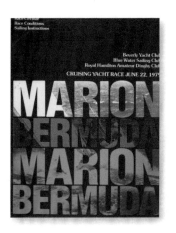

The 1979 Race

Karina was among the 128 teams that started the 1979 race on Friday June 22.
In *Karina's* log, winds were recorded from the south-southwest blowing at 15 knots.
Some boats saw much higher winds that Friday—approaching 25 knots in some cases.

By Monday the 25th, the wind had built to 30 knots, with gusts to 40 out of the northeast. It was then that many in the fleet, including *Karina*, reached the Gulf Stream. Well after the race, the successful Marion-Bermuda skipper Ron Noonan of Westport, MA said of the '79 race:

"We weren't in a survival storm, but we were in a front where the winds were blowing about 30 knots continuously and, of course, in the [Gulf] Stream they were blowing much stronger. The seas built to 15 to 20 feet and the boat was over on its ear. We almost went electrically dead because the boat was heeled so much… I think if a helicopter went by on the fourth day out and they asked for volunteers to leave I would have lost half the crew." [23]

There was no loss of life, and no significant injuries were reported, but two yachts were dismasted and 14 retired from the race due to the heavy conditions. At around noon on Monday the 25th, when Jack Braitmayer made the 30-knot entry in his logbook, the mainmast of *Orion*, a heavy Cheoy Lee Offshore 41 ketch broke in half at the spreader, collapsed, and the butt came out of the mast step fitting on the deck.[24] The crew had to lash the damaged rigging down so that it wouldn't slam against the boat and damage the hull. They set the mizzen staysail halyard as a temporary mizzen forestay (since the triatic stay running from the mizzen masthead to the main masthead was gone), and managed to get to Bermuda under jury rig and engine.

Seven hours later, in 22 knots of wind, the mainmast on the Bermuda yacht *Crescendo II*, a Cal 39, went over the side after buckling at the lower spreader.[25] At that point, *Crescendo II* was well ahead of *Orion* and racing well; she was only 90 nautical miles northeast of Bermuda when the spar failed. The crew strapped the boom and loose rigging

to the boat and motored to Bermuda and into Hamilton harbor. In their official report to the organizers, they said:

"It should be noted that the dismasting occurred when both wind and seas were easing. We had experienced steady winds of 26-36 knots for many hours Sunday and Monday, [the] 24th and 25th, but no heavy squalls (a few light squalls reached a maximum of 40-42 knots on those days). At the time of dismasting the crew were having a steak dinner—on deck—and were on a close reach under heavy reacher (7 oz.) and fully reefed main, debating increasing sail in the lightening conditions."

The report goes on to compliment the organizers for a well-run race, and if not for one defective rigging bolt, *Crescendo II* could have been a contender for a trophy.

Elsewhere in the fleet, the Hinckley Bermuda 40 *Whitecaps* broke a spreader. According to a report in *Yachting*, crewmember Ed White was hoisted up the mast "to capture the flogging spar." [26]

Gabriella, a McCurdy & Rhodes custom ketch owned, skippered and navigated by Henry Clayman of Marblehead, Massachusetts was first to finish, first overall on corrected time, and first in Class B. It was *Gabriella's* first race and she finished in 3 days and 23 hours, a fast passage and course record that would stand until 1987. The Bermuda Chance 39 *Asteroid*, owned and sailed by A.E. Doughty and his family and a repeatedly successful Marion-Bermuda competitor, was third across the line and won the inaugural family trophy. The *Boston Globe* took note of this new aspect of the Marion-Bermuda Race:

"[The Marion-Bermuda Race…[is] the type of race that is attracting more attention in all parts

Elaine St. James photo

Dave Kingery (right) receives the Robert N. Bavier Jr. Trophy from YACHTING's Editor Tony Gibbs, at the conclusion of the second Marion (Mass.) to Bermuda Cruising Yacht Race. First winner of the Trophy, Kingery was nominated by the crew of his Columbia 50 for his seamanship in securing the boat's rig after the roller-furling forestay let go at the tack in 25-knot winds and 12-foot seas.

Race founder Dave Kingery was nominated by his crew to receive the first Bavier Trophy in recognition of his exceptional seamanship during the rough 1979 Marion-Bermuda Race.
Image: *Royal Gazette*

of the sailing world…[The] competitive aspects are there. But there's more than that. Much more. Family activities are stressed…there's the Beverly Family Trophy placed in competition to promote family sailing…the thing this race has going for it is the low-key approach." [27]

Fittingly, the first Bavier seamanship trophy was awarded to Dave Kingery. As reported in *Yachting*:

"…aboard Dave Kingery's Columbia 50 *Keramos*, the headstay let go at the tack fitting while the boat was beating through eight-to-12-foot seas. Fast action preserved the mast by heading off, but a jagged armory of hardware comprised of rod headstay and shards of the slotted furling spar flailed aloft, with bits of the jib tangled in the standing and running rigging. Kingery led the crew in securing gear on deck, rigging a halyard as a temporary stay, cutting away the fragments of the genoa

and tying of [sic] the broken furling device. All this was accomplished amid continuing 25-knot winds, and the 52-year-old Kingery himself spent much of the time in a bosun's chair at spreader level." [28]

Jack Westerbeke, CEO of the eponymous marine engine and generator manufacturer, sailed his Tartan 37 *Isolde* in this race. He and his crew had a mechanical complication right at the start. The centerboard wouldn't go down, essential equipment when beating down Buzzards Bay in a Tartan 37 in light air. They were falling behind their class until Jack went below, grabbed a wrench disconnected the centerboard lift mechanism. He then took a hammer and literally beat the board down and into position; one might say into submission. *Isolde* picked up speed and pointed higher into the wind, exited the Bay in good position, and went on to win first in Class D.

The 1979 race was the proof race. It proved that the idea of a Corinthian ocean race from New England to Bermuda was indeed popular and sustainable. The number of entry applications continued to exceed expectations. It proved that challenging wind and sea conditions would test cruising yachts and their crews, but wouldn't break them. All reached Bermuda safely, or made the prudent decision to return to Marion and try again in a couple of years. The 1979 race also was proof of viable and efficient race organizations ashore. Committees were highly functional and knew what they were doing.

The Selection Committee was a good example. Like other well-run ocean races, the Selection Committee was (and still is) tasked with setting strict entry standards. Yachts had to be inspected for seaworthiness, equipped with the best offshore safety gear, and each crew had to include experienced blue water sailors trained to deal with offshore emergencies. The Committee also was charged with determining whether applicant crews and their boats

Jack Westerbeke's *Isolde* beats out of Buzzards Bay at the start of the 1979 Marion-Bermuda Race, centerboard finally down and pointing well to windward.
Photo: Jack Westerbeke

Nature calls for a crewman drying out when the weather finally cleared during the 1979 race. Photo: Jack Braitmayer

applicant was not accepted, even though the committee had accepted another Tartan 38:

"…the [accepted] boat was indeed 'fitted out for comfortable cruising' and…was not used primarily for racing…The owner certified that the yacht was teak-finished throughout below decks (including the forecabin) that it has in fact been used for cruising more than racing under his ownership, and that his crew is of an average age of 46 and have all cruised with him on his yacht."

Fantasia and the committee were determined to enforce the focus of Marion-Bermuda, clearly articulated in a press release announcing the 1979 race:

"This race is specifically designed for offshore cruising yachts with cruising-style crews as the guidelines indicate. To further ensure that entries fit this category it will be required that they certify that all aboard are amateurs, that there is no commercial intent, and that the yacht and captain are not primarily focused on racing." [30]

met the standards of "Corinthian" and "cruising," in many cases not an easy task. In a letter to one skipper who had hoped to enter his new Tartan 38 in the race, Selection Committee member Joe Fantasia wrote:

"The Race Committee, in formulating the conditions for the second Marion-Bermuda Cruising Yacht Race, gave much consideration to the comments of participants in the first race. A lot of criticism was directed at the participation of yachts and crews that were more race oriented than cruising oriented." [29]

Fantasia listed several highly specific reasons why this

That they largely succeeded is testament to the resolve of the founders and organizers more broadly.

Perhaps the most encouraging thing about this race for Kingery, Bird and the long-term success of the event was that the Beverly Yacht Club, with its deep social and race organizing capabilities, had become a full sponsor of the race. In 1977, while the Beverly Yacht Club had provided facility and logistics support for the inaugural, it was not a sponsor. By 1979 that had changed. The race no longer was the "Blue Water Cruising Yacht Race." It was incorporated as the "Marion-Bermuda Cruising Yacht Race" and the three clubs operated it on an equal and well-coordinated basis.

The Beverly Yacht coordinated yacht safety inspections, entry registrations, starting line operations, hosted the race yachts in Sippican Harbor, and put on the Marion social events. The Blue Water Sailing Club focused on promoting, organizing, staffing and running the Safety at Sea Symposium. The RHADC handled all activities in Bermuda including recording race results, adjudicating protests, handling post-race inspections, managing prize-giving and arranging and hosting social events. Overseeing all was a Board of Trustees and operating committees populated by members of all three clubs. The race is run this way even today.

The 1981 Race

With 153 yachts on the entry list, 1981 continued the upward trend in race size. On the Marion end, the large fleet and celebratory crowds of skippers, crews and "camp followers" had to be accommodated. The Beverly Yacht Club dedicated their compact campus to the operation, and borrowed space from neighboring Tabor Academy for the pre-race Skippers Meeting. After the finish in Bermuda, the RHADC had to do similar things. The clubhouse and grounds were completely taken over by race operations and events, overflow dock space was arranged at the nearby Royal Bermuda Yacht Club, and the awards ceremonies and celebrations were held at the Hamilton Princess Hotel. The Marion-Bermuda Race had become a major undertaking.

Like 1979, the 1981 race had its rough weather, but also flat calms and sea stories to match. There were 35 "DNFs" (Did Not Finish).

A Sinking and Rescue

Sum senex. Exiguus est morei.
[I am an old man. It is insignificant to die.][31]

So scribbled erudite Arthur Herrington as he lay cramped in a life raft 300 miles into the 1981 Marion-Bermuda race. Several hours earlier Herrington had watched his new 58-foot yacht *Satan's Mercy* sink in the North Atlantic. Providentially he and his 7-man crew survived.[32]

A cold front swept across the fleet on Sunday the 21st into Monday the 22nd. *Satan's Mercy* was already six or seven hours ahead of the fleet. She was well into the Gulf Stream and over half way to Bermuda when the front hit. Herrington said later that they were beating into a 45-knot southerly, with 15-20 foot seas, but making 8 ½ knots through the water. He was off watch and asleep below when at 5:30 AM he was jolted awake as the boat fell off a steep wave and the hull shuddered. Seconds later Bill Boykin shouted down from the helm: "Hey, skipper, get up here! We've got big problems!"

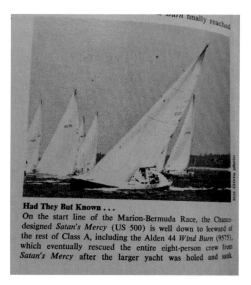

Had They But Known . . .
On the start line of the Marion-Bermuda Race, the Chance-designed *Satan's Mercy* (US 500) is well down to leeward of the rest of Class A, including the Alden 44 *Wind Burn* (9575), which eventually rescued the entire eight-person crew from *Satan's Mercy* after the larger yacht was holed and sank.

The last known photo of *Satan's Mercy* taken at the start of the 1981 Marion-Bermuda Race. The yacht was exceptionally light and had a retractable keel. Photo: *Yachting*

The boat's name is drawn from Wagner's opera *The Flying Dutchman*—"He who trusts the wind, trust's Satan's mercy!" But this was no wind problem—this was a hull problem, and a major one at that. Something had punctured a basketball-size hole in *Satan's Mercy* on the port side forward of the mast and at the water line. She was taking on massive amounts of water. Bilge pumps were useless.

Herrington's new boat was fast and unique. *Satan's Mercy* was co-designed by Herrington himself and naval architect Britton Chance, and built by Concordia Yachts in South Dartmouth, Massachusetts. Her hull was a fiberglass and wood laminate over a foam core. Although published reports are contradictory, it is most likely that *Satan's Mercy* had an unusually large and heavy centerboard or swing keel, and a retractable spade rudder. Herrington lived on Gibson Island just north of Annapolis on the western shore of the Chesapeake Bay. *Satan's Mercy* was designed and built with Chesapeake Bay conditions in mind. James Holechek of the *Baltimore Sun* wrote: "She was a state-of-the-art cruising boat…She was not designed or built as an all-out racing machine. With her radical retractable spade rudder and centerboard up, the 58-foot cutter would glide along [in]18 inches of water—an ideal boat for the Chesapeake." [33] *Satan's Mercy* was big, new, and high-tech. But none of that mattered in the early morning of June 21, 1981.

Herrington waded through the rising knee-deep water in the cabin to the companionway. When he came up he could see why Boykin had hollered. In addition to the hole in the hull, the mast had broken seven feet above the deckhouse. *Satan's Mercy* was in peril. He mobilized the crew and attempted to stem the flood of water into the boat. The *Baltimore Sun* reported:

"Sails were draped over the outside of the hull to let the water pressure seal the sail against the opening,

but the wild rising-falling action of the boat made that impossible. 'A lot of ideas of shoving something in the hole are, quite frankly, poppycock. The first decision I had to make involved the eight men aboard the boat, and you've got to get them off into a life raft without panic.' Herrington said."

The crew did deploy their eight-man raft, and activated their EPRIB. Within an hour of the first shuddering impact, Herrington's boat sank. The EPIRB signal was picked up by an airline pilot passing overhead—in those days EPIRB signals were routed through commercial airliners—and approximately 10 hours later the raft was spotted by a United States Coast Guard C-130 deployed from North Carolina. The C-130 broadcasted a request for assistance on VHF-16, and another Marion-Bermuda yacht *Wind Burn,* an Alden 44 also racing in Class A and then 25 nautical miles away to the south, responded. She dropped sails and motored back towards the life raft's position. The C-130 broadcasted updated raft positions every 30 minutes over the VHF. It took the rescue boat five hours to reach the raft. At last Herrington and his seven crewmates were hauled aboard *Wind Burn* by skipper Bob Biebel and his five crew. According to Boykin, the overmanned *Wind Burn* returned to racing, but when the wind died and the vessel "ran out of beer" they withdrew and motored to Bermuda.

Herrington maintained that the *Satan's Mercy* loss was likely due to his very fast boat colliding with a semi-submerged heavy object in heavy weather. His crew, and other competitors, had reported seeing logs and debris in the water during the 1981 race, possibly washed off the deck of a large vessel. It's possible one such log punctured the hull when she dropped off the wave. The truth lies at the bottom of the Atlantic.

Some have argued that *Satan's Mercy* was not a cruising

Heavy Weather Sailing in 1979 and 1981

boat, but an untested racing machine. The Entry Committee felt otherwise. It may have been a radical boat, but with a well-appointed interior (including three enclosed heads), Joe Fantasia and his committee had determined that while the boat was different, it wasn't a boat designed primarily to race.

Karina's log book shows that by Tuesday night during that race, the wind had fallen way off, and by Wednesday there was no wind at all. After taking a refreshing swim around their becalmed boat, *Karina* and 36 other boats surrendered to the inevitable, and joined *Wind Burn* in withdrawing from the race. *Karina* motored on to Bermuda and to a welcoming RHADC. By then *Satan's Mercy* was under a mile of water at the bottom of the Atlantic.

As Marion-Bermuda grew in stature it also attracted several sailors who were famous for reasons other than sailing. The globally-recognized CBS News anchorman Walter Cronkite sailed his 42' Westsail yawl *Wyntje* in the 1981 race. A self-acknowledged sailing amateur, Cronkite invited America's Cup veteran Gary Jobson to be his Tactician aboard *Wyntje*. This, of course, presented Entry Chairman Joe Fantasia and the Selection Committee with a quandary—to what extent was having Gary Jobson, a professional sailor at the top of the sport, aboard a Marion-Bermuda Race yacht a violation of the Corinthian spirit of the Marion-Bermuda Race?

A sailor with the public stature of Walter Cronkite obviously would be good for race publicity, but Jobson was obviously a pro. *SAIL* magazine reported:

"Perhaps the most photographed entrant was *Wyntje*, Walter Cronkite's Westsail 42. Tactician for the former anchorman was Gary Jobson, who filled the same spot in *Courageous's* last two America's Cup efforts. Jobson sailed the race despite efforts by the race organizers just days before the start to

A sailor from *Karina* takes a swim during the calm following the storm in the 1981 race. Photo: Jack Braitmayer

have him barred on grounds he was a professional. At Cronkite's suggestion, Jobson wrote a one-sentence letter stating he would not use the race for any commercial purposes—a move that apparently fulfilled the "amateur only" stipulation in the racing instructions." [34]

Fantasia and his committee handled the matter with care and diplomacy, ensuring that Jobson sailed to Bermuda aboard *Wyntje* in 1981 as an unpaid amateur; at least for that race. There were grumblings in the fleet, but given

Bob Biebel, skipper/owner of the yacht *Wind Burn* accepting the Bavier Trophy from YACHTING's Editor Tony Gibbs.

It surprised no one the following Saturday when Bob Biebel received the Bavier Trophy for outstanding seamanship and sportsmanship in the Marion-to-Bermuda Cruising Race. The only major yachting trophy

Bob Biebel of *Wind Burn* receiving the 1981 Bavier Trophy for seamanship in 1981. Biebel and his crew rescued all hands from *Satan's Mercy*, adrift in a life raft after their yacht had sunk. Photo: *Yachting*

Wally Feldman aboard *Bright Star* takes a deck bath during the calmer stages of the 1981 Marion-Bermuda Race. Photo: *SAIL*

that Cronkite withdrew from the race due to a lack of wind close to Bermuda, there were no lasting hard feelings.

In a post-race interview, Cronkite described himself as "A good seaman, but not a racer like the rest of these guys." He said: "I'm no novice, but I'm not a racer. This [the 1981 Marion-Bermuda Race] was my first real race. I had a ball." This was good for the organizers to hear, and accurately captured the spirit of the race.

Bob Biebel and *Wind Burn* won the 1981 Bavier trophy for their prompt and well-executed rescue of Herrington

and his crew. A.J. Shatkin in his Swan 36 sloop *Edelweiss* won on corrected time, and the 53' Schmidt sloop *Sly Mongoose IV* owned and sailed by J. D. Cochran was first to finish in 4 days, 6 hours and 54 minutes. Herb Marcus on *Silkie* was again the fastest shorthanded yacht and winner of Class B on corrected time.

The Beverly Yacht Club

The Beverly Yacht Club has always managed the Marion-Bermuda Race starting line, and since 1979 has co-sponsored the race along with the RHADC and the Blue Water Sailing Club. The club was founded in 1872, making the Beverly one of the oldest yacht clubs in the country. It was founded by a group of small boat racers who broke away from the Eastern Yacht Club in Marblehead.[35] Eastern had been organized only two years earlier, but had adopted a club rule that small yachts, those with waterlines less than 30 feet, were not eligible to race in the club's regattas.

Edward Burgess, the most celebrated yacht designer of his time (and father of W. Starling Burgess who was equally, if not more, accomplished than his father), founded the Beverly Yacht Club with a handful of friends specifically to encourage and organize racing for smaller yachts. The club motto is *I itus ama altum alii teneant*: "Others seek the deep, I prefer the shallow" refers to the founders' love of coastal racing in small vessels. In certain respects, the motives behind the founding of BYC foreshadowed those behind the Marion-Bermuda Race; BYC would encourage small boat racing in the age of ever-larger yachts, and much later Marion-Bermuda would encourage Corinthian ocean racing in the age of increasing professionalism in sailing.

BYC organized its first regatta off Beverly, Massachusetts in the summer of 1872. The fleet consisted of 10 catboats and one sloop. The club continued to sponsor small boat races off Beverly, Marblehead, Boston, and even off Monument Beach (at the northeast head of Buzzards Bay and 60 miles to the south of Beverly itself) for the next 23 years without having a clubhouse to call home. By 1895 it became clear that a new home was required. Race participation in the Monument Beach regattas had been growing, possibly due to more consistent and challenging winds that funnel

ABOVE: The Wings Neck Station of the Beverly Yacht Club circa 1899. The Beverly Yacht Club Buzzards Bay station moved from here to Sippican Harbor in 1912. From: Rosbe, Arcadia Publishing

LEFT: Edward Burgess was the first Commodore of the Beverly Yacht Club. The club was founded in 1872 by a group of sailors committed to small boat racing in an era of a trend towards larger yachts and professional crews, a foreshadow of the role the Beverly Yacht Club would play in launching the Marion-Bermuda Race a century later. From: Rosbe, Arcadia Publishing

up Buzzards Bay. The members chose to settle into a rented shore-side station with a wharf on the Cape Cod side of the bay at Wing's Neck. The club then purchased the Wing's Neck station in 1899. The BYC had transitioned from a sailing association into a proper yacht club.

BYC might have remained at Wings Neck had it not been for the success of an enterprising New Yorker named August Belmont Jr. who had moved to Cape Cod. This was an age of gargantuan civil engineering accomplishments like the Suez Canal (1869), Brooklyn Bridge (1883), Eiffel Tower (1889), and the first underground mass transit rail line (the Budapest subway, opened in 1896), Belmont had organized financing for New York City's first subway line (1904). Following five failed attempts by predecessors, Belmont bought a charter

The present home of the Beverly Yacht Club on Water Street in Marion, MA on Sippican Harbor. The members purchased the building and substantial wharf in 1955 and have updated and expanded the clubhouse to accommodate social and sailing operations.
From Rosbe, Arcadia Publishing

to build a canal that would link Buzzards Bay with Cape Cod Bay. He hired William Parsons who had engineered the New York City subway, as chief engineer. They launched a project first envisioned in writing by Miles Standish in 1623, which was to connect the Scusett and Manomet rivers across a mile-wide isthmus of dry land that joined Cape Cod to the mainland. Dredging began in 1909, and over the next five years the massive steam-driven diggers dumped millions of tons of slurry into northern Buzzards Bay immediately off Monument Beach. BYC's regatta area was ruined.

In January, 1912 the membership had enough and decided to move across Buzzards Bay to the western, or mainland, shore. They bought land on Ruggle's Point on the northern side of the entrance to Sippican Harbor and across from the waterside town of Marion. They built a respectable clubhouse on Ruggle's Point and got back to sailboat racing. Racing thrived on Buzzards Bay in the early 20th century, and BYC was at the center of the phenomenon.

Since arriving on Wing's Neck, the club members stimulated the development of some of the most successful small boats of the era, including several catboat one designs, as

well as the remarkable series of boats designed and built for Buzzards Bay by Nathaniel Herreshoff including the Buzzards Bay 15s, 25s and 30s. The collaboration between Herreshoff and the Buzzards Bay sailors reached its apogee with the H12½, the "Buzzards Bay Boys Boat", first launched in 1912 the year the BYC moved to Sippican. More than five hundred of these boats have been built of wood since its debut, and derivative designs in both wood and fiberglass (the H 12½, the Haven 12½, the "Doughdish" and "Bullseye") are still in production today. It is one of the most beautiful and successful boat designs of all time, and remains a popular racing class at the Beverly Yacht Club.

After merging with the failing Sippican Yacht Club, BYC moved its station farther into Sippican Harbor, including a brief stay at Barden's Boat Yard on Water Street (both the yard and club nearly destroyed by Hurricane Carol in 1954). Finally, in 1955 the membership bought an historic building that came with a substantial wharf at the end of Main and Water streets in Marion itself. This is the club's location today.

In 1972, the Beverly Yacht Club displayed its capacity for innovation and collaboration when it launched the massively successful Buzzards Bay Regatta with the New Bedford Yacht Club. The BBR has become the nation's best-attended racing regatta, often with over 400 yachts competing. When Dave Kingery approached the Beverly Yacht Club officers in 1975 with the proposal to co-sponsor his and Dickie Bird's Marion-Bermuda race concept, it's no wonder that the BYC bridge decided to take a wait-and-see attitude given what was on their plate with the new Buzzards Bay Regatta. BYC did step forward to help Kingery, Bird, the Blue Water Sailing Club and the RHADC, assisting with registration, staging, and starting line management. The Marion-Bermuda Race would never have put to sea without BYC in 1977, and when the Beverly Yacht Club became a full sponsor in 1979, Marion-Bermuda found a permanent home in the USA.

Kathleen of Marion has been a frequent competitor. Owned by James Feeney, the custom 72' yawl won Class A in 2007, and her navigator Walt Lacey won the Navigator's Trophy for first on corrected time using celestial navigation. Photo: Ray Cullum

Becoming a Great Ocean Race Through the 1980s

"Record breaking…" often appears in the accounts of the Marion-Bermuda race in the 1980s. J. Cochran's *Sly Mongoose IV* won back-to-back line honors in 1981 and 1983, a record never since matched. Paul D'Arcy and his family crew aboard *Runaway* set a course record in 1987 that had stood since H.P. Clayman's fast passage in 1979 with *Gabriella* only to have Bermudian Warren Brown's *War Baby* break it in 1989. Most importantly for Corinthian ocean racing, the Marion-Bermuda Race broke its own records for number of boats at the starting line each successive year. In 1989 the race reached its all-time high with 169 boats starting, a record that still stands today.

Organizers resolved important matters ashore in the early 1980s. The 1977 and 1979 races were loose collaborations among the three yacht clubs. In 1980 that changed. In August of that year the Marion-Bermuda Race was incorporated as The Marion-Bermuda Cruising Yacht Race Association, Inc. in the Commonwealth of Massachusetts and also was qualified as a nonprofit entity under federal tax code. Organizers also settled on a rating system that resolved some of the friction caused by the somewhat unclear boundaries of their earlier handicap schemes. In 1983 they adopted the International Measurement System (IMS), an early version of predicted performance handicap systems, which was developed initially by members of the Cruising Club of America working with MIT engineers and widely used today.[36]

The 1983 Race

The 1983 race of 127 yachts encountered light air at the start. It turned out that the race essentially was decided within the first several hours. *SAIL* magazine said, "The strategy used to get out of Buzzards Bay was key. There was light air, and conditions favored local knowledge."[37] Class D had to wait through a 30-minute start delay due to a lack of wind. Ron Noonan and his 1977 custom Bristol 40 sloop *Wildflower* made their Marion-Bermuda debut in 1983. Hailing from Westport, Massachusetts, and based in Marion, this Beverly Yacht Club member and retired Naval officer used his local knowledge of the Bay to good effect. By the time the committee boat fired the warning gun for *Wildflower's* Class G, a gentle southwesterly was stirring. Noonan chose to tack down the eastern shore of the Bay to get tidal eddies and a slightly better breeze far from the lee of the western shore. His tactics at sea also proved perfect. A front stalled over the fleet on Tuesday, but Noonan had chosen the western side of the rhumb line and was an early winner of a breeze that finally filled in from the west. *Wildflower* reached back to the rhumb line while those on the line or east of it had to beat into Bermuda. He and *Wildflower* won first overall in the 1983 race.

Ron Noonan's *Wildflower*s (a Bristol 40, then a Sabre 402 in the years 1999 and later) rank with Herb Marcus's *Silkie* as the most successful Marion-Bermuda yachts. Noonan won a total of 12 trophies in his seven campaigns that stretched from 1983 through 2001 (with only a handful of races missed), including an overall win repeat in 1993 and a near three-peat in 1995 when he was edged out by Richard Leather in *Columbine* by only 29 minutes (corrected time). Fast, well-sailed boats that are smaller than fleet averages like the *Wildflower*s can do well in distance races like Marion-Bermuda. Noonan told an interviewer at the Bermuda *Royal Gazette* in 1995:

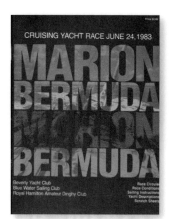

"...the boats run from about 65 feet down to 35 feet or whatever and we tend to be in the smaller boat section. The larger boats may be 90 miles to 100 miles ahead and they can be in an entirely different weather system. ...I've had situations where it has worked to my advantage or my disadvantage. A couple of times I remember being right off Bermuda and being able to count the lights of the hotels and drifting. Then there's been times where the big boats run into light air and we carried heavy air in like [in 1993]."

Ron Noonan and *Wildflower* lead the Class G boats out of Buzzards Bay in 1991. The Bristol 40 won first overall in 1983 and 1993. Photo: 1995 Marion-Bermuda Race book

Measured by the total number of trophies won, Ron Noonan remains the most successful skipper in Marion-Bermuda Race history.

The 1985 Race

Investigative journalist Geraldo Rivera entered his first of many Marion-Bermuda races in 1985. New to ocean racing at the time, Rivera sailed his Gulfstar 44 *New Wave* to a provisional 6th place finish in his class. He sailed with retired  TV reporter Hugh Downs, recording a video documentary of the trip that was broadcast nationally on "60 Minutes."

Downs was a very experienced blue water sailor, and served as celestial navigator. Rivera and the fleet had light air for the first several days of the race, but on Wednesday, as the bulk of the fleet approached Bermuda, a warm front moved across the racecourse. Heavy squalls punctuated by humid calms rolled through. It was heavy going, but for boats who got the wind first, it mattered. *SAIL* magazine reported:

> "All of the boats that won class honors and special trophies went at least 80 miles to the west, where winds were fair, while boats that hugged the rhumb line suffered through a succession of calms and storms." [38]

For Rivera, from Wednesday on the race was a reefed close reach sprint in heavy air all the way to the finish. Unfortunately for *New Wave*, way back in Marion and seconds before the starting gun, a yawl immediately in front of and crossing Rivera's bow had caught the aft end of its mizzen boom in *New Wave's* bow pulpit. Although both

Geraldo Rivera is one of a number of sailor-celebrities who have entered the Marion-Bermuda Race. Here he is interviewed at the RHADC by race volunteer Wendy Cullum in 2003. Photo: Ray Cullum

yachts were on starboard tack and claimed priority, the Race Committee determined that the collision was Rivera's fault. When the *New Wave* crew arrived in Hamilton, they learned that they'd been disqualified. The documentary shows Rivera and Downs accepting the ruling gracefully. Geraldo Rivera has since become something of a fixture in the race, campaigning a series of his own yachts, including one of IBM co-founder Thomas Watson's later *Palawans* (rechristened *Voyager*).

In the 1985 race, two yachts, *Carioca* and *Fleetwing*, were dismasted by especially violent storms, and *Fleetwing* eventually had to be abandoned. The overall winner was a small but extraordinarily well-sailed yacht hailing from Alabama named *Pirate*. The Bob Bavier trophy for outstanding seamanship went to *Carioca* and the Air-Sea Rescue Team of U.S. Naval Air Station Bermuda for their work assisting the crew of *Fleetwing*.

The 1987 Race

Sailed under the new IMS handicap system, the 1987 race was a sailor's race. The fastest on record up to that time, it began on June 19 with 149 boats becalmed off Marion. The fleet included Sir John Swan, Premier of Bermuda and an "avid cruising sailor" expectantly awaiting his first Marion-Bermuda Race start.[39] Conditions changed. As the smaller classes came to the line, a New England "smoky sou'wester" filled in and anemometers read 25 knots and more. Jack Braitmayer's log shows wind readings out of the southwest touching 30 knots before the boat left Buzzards Bay. The race was a rhumbline sail to Bermuda.

Paul D'Arcy's 59-foot Hood/Maas cutter *Runaway* took line honors, completing the race in 80 hours. *Legend*, the winner of First Overall, also took the Class B silverware along with the Family Trophy. Sailed by Kevin Carse and his family, *Legend* was a particularly satisfactory winner for the race organizers. *SAIL* magazine said:

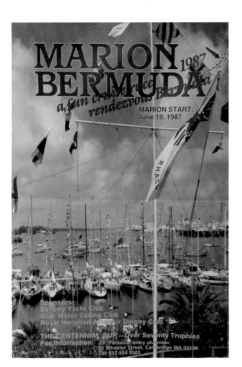

A promotional poster for the 1987 Marion-Bermuda race. Marketing the race has been the responsibility of the Operating Committee. Photo: RHADC Archives

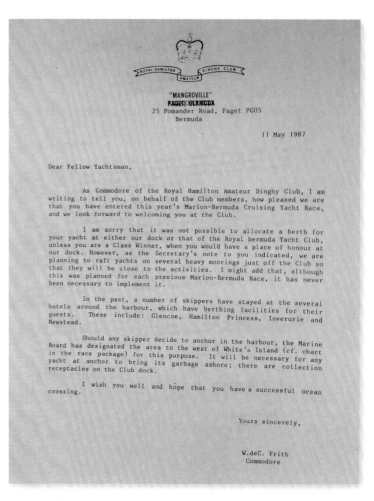

By the late 1980s, the Marion-Bermuda Race fleet had grown to a size that the RHADC had to assist skippers in finding alternate berthing options while in Hamilton Harbor. Photo: RHADC Archives

"Amidst talk in Bermuda of a few questionable boats sailing with empty water tanks, missing interior furniture, changed steering ratios, taller spars added, and grand-prix style continuous rail-sitting by some crews, the Carse's success was all the more gratifying because it reaffirmed the original concept of the event, a 'family cruiser race.'"[40]

Kevin Carse proved once again that a smaller boat, well-sailed, could find great success in the Marion-Bermuda Race.

The 1989 Race

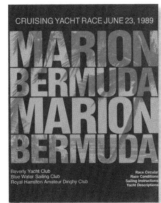

Perhaps the most famous yacht/skipper pairing ever to compete in the Marion-Bermuda Race won line honors in 1989. Bermudian Warren Brown sailed his *War Baby* to a new course record, beating 162 competitors, the largest racing fleet in Marion-Bermuda history.

Brown bought *War Baby* from Ted Turner, the American media entrepreneur, ocean racer, and America's Cup skipper. Later Brown also bought the 12-meter *American Eagle* from Turner. The two men were close, at least in the business of boats.

War Baby is a 1971 Sparkman & Stephens design. Launched as *Dora 4* she was campaigned on the Great Lakes by her original owner. Turner bought her, added a taller mast, rechristened the boat *Tenacious*, and won almost as often as he sailed. Turner said in a *Sailing World* magazine article: "Why do you think my own racing yacht is named *Tenacious*, dummy? Because I never quit. I've got a bunch of flags on my boat, but they're ain't no white flags. I never give up." [41]

Turner and *Tenacious* are perhaps best known as the winners of the 1979 Fastnet, the infamous race that capsized so many yachts and cost the lives of 15 sailors. Their most intense competition in the early 1980s came from *Running Tide*, *Ondine* and *Kialoa*, which along with *Tenacious* repeatedly surfaced as first-to-finish or Class A winners in the world's top competitions like the Southern Ocean racing Conference (S.O.R.C.) series.

When he bought *Tenacious* from Turner, Brown renamed her *War Baby*. This was one of a series of Warren Brown 'War Babys.' In an interview in February, 2015, Allan Williams, former Commodore of the Royal Hamilton Amateur Dinghy Club and crewman aboard

War Baby when they set the Marion-Bermuda course record, surmised that Brown named his yachts for War Baby Fox, a Bermudian boat builder. War Baby Fox built Bermuda cedar dinghies on St. David's Island, and Brown's first boat was a cedar dinghy he named *War Baby*. Further email correspondence with Brown's family and others confirms that Brown did in fact name his boats in memory of War Baby Fox.

Brown was an accomplished Bermuda businessman. He was forced to become familiar with the perils of the sea at a very early age. As a three-month-old, *enroute* to Bermuda from New York with his mother Mabel on the *RMS Fort Victoria*, he was rescued along with 269 passengers and 165 crew after it was rammed in thick fog by the *SS Algonquin*. [42]

After graduating from Yale, he went into and grew the family business (Archie Brown & Son clothiers on Front St.). He also established a publishing business.

Brown was an ocean racer, expedition sailor and an Olympian. He represented Bermuda in the Olympics as

a competitor (1972) and team coach (1992). He logged more than 300,000 miles on his *War Baby* ocean racers. He was Commodore of the Royal Bermuda Yacht Club, sailed in twenty Newport to Bermuda races in eleven different boats, including four he owned. He raced in the Fastnet eight times. He also was an

Bermudian Warren Brown at the start of the 1989 Marion-Bermuda Race in *War Baby*. Brown won on elapsed time. A veteran ocean racer and blue water sailor, Brown was awarded the coveted Cruising Club of America's Blue Water Medal. Photo: Warren Brown family

War Baby (formerly *Tenacious*) won the 1989 Marion-Bermuda Race and set a course record. Photo: Warren Brown family

accomplished high latitude sailor, sailing as far north as Spitzbergen, Norway, and twice to the Antarctic for which he was awarded the Cruising Club of America's Blue Water Medal in 1988. Paul Doughty said: "He was a fantastic guy, a true explorer, adventurer, yachtsman and sailor. He … survived a hurricane in the Gulf Stream …and he also … did work for the Chilean navy and knew everybody you could ever conceive of at the top end of yachting." Ted Turner was one of Brown's acquaintances. Allan Williams was quoted: "He had wonderful opportunities, which he took total advantage of. He was a great guy to sail with and I did a Marion to Bermuda Race with him years ago when we broke the record." When he died on Christmas Day, 2014, Warren Brown was 85.

War Baby's trip to the Marion-Bermuda starting line was interesting as well. Rives Potts is an America's Cup veteran, ocean racer (including the 1997 Marion-Bermuda Race aboard his famous *Carina*) and recent past Commodore of the New York Yacht Club. He wrote the following in an email:

"I believe it was perhaps in 1989 that Warren brought War Baby to our yard…Pilots Point Marina, in Westbrook, CT…. to prepare her for a go at the Marion-Bermuda Race record. I was manager of PPM at the time.

Warren and I were good friends and he had brought *War Baby* to me several times over the years to modify or upgrade various systems, rigging, and expedition features. I had sailed on his *War Baby*, with Ted Turner, when she was called *Tenacious*, for several years in the late 70's, including the 1979 Fastnet Race. I knew the boat pretty well. We had installed a new keel on her in December 1980 in time for her to race in the 1981 SORC. She left in an ice storm from CT in January 1981.

In 1989, Warren sailed the boat from the Caribbean to PPM in the early spring to get her ready for the Marion-Bermuda Race that June. He had successfully campaigned her in the Caribbean regattas that winter under the CSA rating rule, which measures the boat's LOA from the transom to the forward-most part of the deck. The CSA rule measured *War Baby* to be 60' LOA. At the time, the Marion-Bermuda Race was being raced under the relatively new IMS rating, so Warren needed an IMS certificate. Warren engaged an IMS measurer to take the appropriate measurements so that *War Baby* could race in the upcoming race.

The IMS measurer came to PPM to take certain measurements while the boat was out of the water getting her final bottom touch ups before the race. Warren called me a few days later and told me that the measurer had found *War Baby* to actually be 60'-9" LOA, which put her over the 60' maximum allowed by the race. He had already started notifying his crew that *War Baby* would not be doing the race. He was very disappointed.

I went out and measured the boat myself and found that on deck, she measured 60'-0", but the extended aluminum hull bulwarks extended out another 9" which is where the IMS rule dictated the LOA be measured.

I called Warren and asked him if I could make the boat 60' LOA by the IMS rule and get it re-measured by the official measurer, would he allow me to do so? He approved, and within a few hours I skill-sawed the bow off and shaped and welded an aluminum plate across the bow and painted it…so that one may not even notice it…except for a little flattened nose. It measured exactly 60'-0".

Becoming a Great Ocean Race Through the 1980s

Warren did the race and I believe he broke the elapsed time record that year.

I mounted the cut-off proboscis and sent it to Warren. I saw it years later on his wall in his office in Bermuda.

Sometimes things work out well. Everyone was happy with the outcome of this episode in *War Baby's* fabled history." [43]

War Baby was one of a series of very fast Bermuda boats to compete in Marion-Bermuda in the late 1980s and early 1990s. E. Kirkland "Kirk" Cooper sailed *Alphida* in 1991, winning line honors but leaving Brown's elapsed time record intact. However, in 1993 he and *Alphida* raced again, and broke the *War Baby* record by a razor thin 21 seconds.

As of this writing, the Marion-Bermuda Race has been sailed twenty times. Bermuda boats have been first-to-finish five times, or on average once every four races. [44]

SAIL magazine shipped an entire crew of editors and writers aboard *Boston Light* in the 1989 race. The boat is a Skye 51 and was skippered by Patience Wales. The team wrote a feature article titled "So We Didn't Win". [45] What is clear from the article is that they sailed in the race for fun. They didn't do particularly well, but they enjoyed themselves and they got to Bermuda. They were up against serious Corinthian competition, including Warren Brown and *War Baby*. The race had some rough weather. The crew aboard *Boston Light* sailed a conservative race. Wales wrote: "My premise was that cruisers protect their boats; racers push on regardless." In contrast, the eventual overall winner took an entirely different approach. Quoted in the same article, Thomas Plummer, navigator aboard *Yukon Jack*, said: "…I looked around at the heaving Gulf Stream seas and said, 'If we were careful seamen we'd slow this boat down, but if we want to win we'd better keep going as we are.'" Keep going they did, and *Yukon Jack* won the 1989 race on corrected time.

As of this writing, 1989 was the only Marion-Bermuda race in which a competitor died of sailing-related injuries. Thousands of competitors have sailed in well over one thousand yachts in the more than twenty times this event has run. One fatality is tragic, and all of us in sailing and those involved in the race wished it hadn't happened, and certainly hope that it never happens again. The most accurate report on what happened comes from the archives in the official report on the incident. Dated July 3, 1989, it was authored by Sydney J. Peerless, M.D. and sent to Tom Farquhar, Race Committee Chairman. [46] At about 2300 hours on June 25, 1989, Kenneth J. Baxter was at the helm of the Canadian entry *Bellatrix*, a custom McCurdy & Rhodes designed 44-foot aluminum sloop. Watchmate Dr. Donald Hill, Chief of Pediatrics at the University of British Columbia in Vancouver, was in the cockpit. *Bellatrix* was in the Gulf Stream, about 300 miles north of Bermuda, and broad reaching at 6.5—8.5 knots on port tack under mainsail alone. According to Peerless:

"The boom was held out by a mechanical vang and a multiple purchase preventer, which was attached to the boom by a heavy steel clamshell. The yacht was under good control, but steering had become difficult in confused seas of the Gulf Stream… At approximately 2320 hours, the vessel healed [sic] heavily to starboard, there was a loud crash and the vessel rounded up on the starboard tack. Myself, Michael Peerless and Drew Peerless rushed out of the cabin to find the cockpit full of water, the helmsman…holding onto the wheel, the binnacle broken off at the pedestal, and its guardrail twisted off, the main steering compass gone, and Donald Hill lying prone across the lee (port) cockpit combing, his head in the lee scuppers and his pelvis and legs in the cockpit proper."

Corinthian Resolve: The Story of the Marion-Bermuda Race

Marion—Bermuda Race

1989 race entry *Boston Light* was crewed entirely by employees of *SAIL* magazine. The trip resulted in a feature article in the September, 1989 issue. Photo: *SAIL*

Hill had been hit in the head by the boom in the uncontrolled jibe. The vang and preventer had failed. Peerless, himself a neurosurgeon, tended to Hill's head injuries as best he could. He then activated his LORAN, and issued a "Mayday" on the single-sideband radio. Two Marion-Bermuda Race boats *Merry Kate* and *Sea Mouse* responded, as did a Soviet research vessel, the *Akademic Vernadsky.* Peerless wrote: "Recognizing the seriousness of the injury to the crewman, Donald Hill, I requested the Soviet ship to come to our aid in that they had a physician and medical facilities on board."

The *Akademic Vernadsky* reached *Bellatrix* at about 0330 on the 26th, and maneuvered alongside the yacht as best they could in the seaway. *Bellatrix* took a beating as she worked against the side of the Soviet ship. Peerless wrote:

"At about 0430 hours, after being laced into a canvas and wooden stretcher, crewman Donald Hill

was transferred through a side hatch in the Soviet vessel and I, as a skipper and surgeon, scrambled aboard the Soviet vessel under very difficult conditions. Upon reaching the Soviet ship's hospital, I concluded that Donald Hill had expired."

Akademic Vernadsky took *Bellatrix* in tow, and steamed northwest to Fire Island, NY where they were met by the United States Coast Guard and other officials.

According to the Coast Guard reports and Peerless himself, it is probable that *Bellatrix* was hit by a sudden "rogue" wave in the Gulf Stream. The impact of the wave in the darkness forced the boat into an uncontrolled jibe which broke the preventer. As Race Committee Chairman Tom Farquhar said to the press later: "It's a tragedy... I send my sympathies to the friends and family of the deceased. Offshore racing is inherently risky, which of course by no means lessens this tragedy."

61

Marion-Bermuda Race
Safety-at-Sea Symposia

The Marion-Bermuda Race was early, if not pioneering, in the safety-at-sea seminar movement of the late 1970s and early 1980s. These training seminars are one reason why the Marion-Bermuda Race has been lauded as a safe way for cruising sailors make the 645-nautical mile passage across the Gulf Stream to Bermuda.

Safety-at-Sea symposia were energized by individuals and events. An example of an event was the deadly 1979 Fastnet Race. That catastrophe highlighted the need for better heavy weather and seamanship preparedness among ocean racers. Prominent individuals included Capt. John B. Bonds at the US Yacht Racing Union (later US Sailing) and Director of Navy Sailing at the United States Naval Academy, as well as Richard C. McCurdy who chaired the US Sailing Safety Committee in the early 1980s. Another prominent individual was Prof. David Kingery of the Marion-Bermuda Race.

Prior to the 1977 race, there was no seminar offered to Marion-Bermuda competitors. There had been training seminars for Transpac competitors early on, but in the late 1970s the idea of an organizer pre-race seminar or symposium was a relatively new concept. In 1979, that changed. Five years before Capt. Bonds opened his US Naval Academy safety at sea seminars to the public in Annapolis, Kingery, with help from Joe Fantasia, E.J. Downing and Herb Marcus from the Blue Water Sailing Club organized two separate evening meetings, one in Boston at the Science Museum planetarium on May 14, 1979, the second the following day at the American Museum of Natural History's Hayden Planetarium.[47] They charged $3.00 admission. [48] The agenda for both was simple: A "Tour of the Night Sky," previewing celestial navigation options over the upcoming four-night passage to Bermuda; a general "Navigation Talk" discussing the Gulf Stream, medical and general safety procedures, and a "Heavy Weather Sailing Discussion" covering sail handling

SEMINAR SPEAKERS:

Nick Nicholson — Joe Barr — John Rousmaniere — Robbie Doyle

The speaker line-up for the 1985 Safety-at-Sea Symposium.
Photo: 1987 Marion-Bermuda Race Book

and seamanship strategies in heavy winds.

By 1981 a "Seminar Committee" became part of the overall Marion-Bermuda Race Organizing Committee and for the next four years the program was chaired by Fantasia. Seminars were still held in Boston and New York, but moved to MIT and the Seaman's Church Institute respectively. Later, the New York symposium was convened at the Downtown Athletic Club.

Offshore sailing luminaries like Rod Stephens of Sparkman & Stephens, author Hal Roth, author-racer John Rousmaniere and Capt. Bonds himself gave talks and even moderated the Marion-Bermuda programs. Rousmaniere has moderated Marion-Bermuda symposia as recently as March 2015.

The MIT seminar was particularly interesting in that over the years an in-water component was added as a second day option for attendees, initially held at the MIT boathouse on the Charles River.

In 1989 Fantasia turned the program over to Norman Doelling. By 1999, the New York seminar had been discontinued, but the program

Sailor-author John Rousmaniere moderated the 2015 Safety-at-Sea Symposium held at UMass Boston. Photo: Fran Grenon

The overflow crowd at the 1989 Safety-at-Sea Symposium for the Marion-Bermuda Race. The speaker is Capt. John Bonds, an early advocate and organizer of formal safety and seamanship training. Photo: 1989 Marion-Bermuda Race Book

Audience volunteers trying out an eight-person life raft on the stage at the 2015 Safety-at-Sea Symposium. Photo: Fran Grenon

continued in Boston at MIT, with the in-water component of the program moving to the MIT swimming pool, a far more congenial environment than the Charles River for attendees to learn how to enter a life raft from the water. Blue Water Sailing Club members Paul and Annette Hodess, Paul LaVoie, George Weinert and Allan McLean (who went on to become Executive Director of the race in 2013) were tapped to chair the program in the first decade of the 2000s.

In 2005, the Marion-Bermuda Safety-at-Sea Symposium had become a US Sailing-sanctioned Safety-at-Sea Seminar, finally connecting with the national movement within US Sailing initiated by John Bonds and Dick McCurdy. Skippers, navigators and crewmen planning to enter the Marion-Bermuda Race, the Marblehead to Halifax Race, as well as the Newport Bermuda race were welcomed to the event.

Ed Stott became Chairman of the Symposium in 2013 and moved the program from MIT to the more spacious and convenient University of Massachusetts, Boston campus. The 2015 program was held at UMass Boston as well, and will continue to be there in the foreseeable future. It has

The Safety-at-Sea Symposium organized by the Blue Water Sailing Club for the Marion-Bermuda Race has featured an in-water training component since the early 1980s. Participants learn how to use their personal flotation equipment correctly, how exit a yacht safely, and how to enter a life raft from the water. Photo: Fran Grenon

become a well-attended and highly regarded program. In 2013, registrations exceeded the capacity of the venue, and attendance had to be capped at just over 300 sailors.

Mischievous is a Meriten 65 campaigned by the Massachusetts Maritime Academy.
Donated to the Academy by Charles Cahill, *Mischievous* was first-to-finish in the 2015 race,
clocking a time second only to course record-holder *Lilla* set in the 2011 race. Photo: Fran Grenon

The 1990s: Steady Hands at the Helm

When the Marion-Bermuda Race was invented, Dickie Bird and Dave Kingery had an outsized role in its organization and operation. The historical record shows that they did recognize that others made significant contributions. Kingery mentions that Teddy Gosling in Bermuda, and Joe Fantasia and Leo Fallon were very important in the early years. Dickie Bird talked about the significant contributions made by Coles Diel (RHADC Commodore) and "Shorty" Trimingham, Minister of Tourism in the Bermuda Government, to the success of those early races. Regardless, and as important as many were in the first years of Marion-Bermuda, it was a creature of Kingery and Bird.

That had changed completely by the 1990s. The race was an established and prestigious event, and many top amateur sailors wanted to race in both the Newport Bermuda and Marion-Bermuda races. It became important to be associated with the race, both in Marion and in Bermuda. It had attracted the time and energy of a stable group of overseers on both ends of the course.

The Government of Bermuda had recognized that the Marion-Bermuda Race was a steady contributor to the island's economy and image, particularly among well-heeled Americans. Since its inception in 1977, the Government has contributed its prestige and funds to support the Bermuda end of the race. By the 1990s, the positive impact of the race on Bermuda was clear and Government support expanded considerably. The yacht clubs on either end of the race—Beverly Yacht Club in Marion, and RHADC in Hamilton, were fully committed and engaged. The Blue Water Sailing Club settled in its roles as well. They organized and operated the biennial Safety-at-Sea Symposium held each March prior to the race, and continued to populate the Trustees and Management Committees. Kingery and Bird were still involved, but their supporting cast was a group of Corinthian sailors who cared deeply about their invention, and ensured its permanence among great ocean races.

The 1991 Race

The 1991 race had 117 starters, down from 163 in 1989. There were at least two reasons for the reduced fleet size. First, the US economy (and by extension, Bermuda's) was in a recession. Competitors in the Marion-Bermuda Race are successful people, but not necessarily among the "mega-rich." Recessions matter. The second reason is that in 1990, the Newport Bermuda Race added a "Cruising Class" to its line-up. Since 1983, the Marion-Bermuda Race fleet had been considerably larger than the following year's Newport fleet.[49] That changed in 1990 Newport race. Since 1984, the Newport Race fleets had averaged 120 boats. In 1990, the fleet jumped to 145 with the inclusion of the new cruising class. In 1991, Marion-Bermuda

entries dropped. Although circumstantial, these data suggest that the Newport Bermuda organizers recognized that Dickie Bird and Dave Kingery had been on to something—that cruising sailors can and want to race from New England to Bermuda. Fortunately for both events, the interest among Corinthian and cruising sailors has been great enough to populate both races.

Jack Braitmayer raced his third *Karina*, a Little Harbor 42 sloop, in the 1991 race. His logbook shows that at the start, the breeze was light and out of the east/southeast. By Saturday June 22, the wind had veered to an easterly and the cloud cover had thickened. On the morning of Sunday, the 23rd, a strong frontal system crossed over *Karina*. At 0945, winds had backed into the west and heavy rain lashed the fleet. Gusts reached 30 knots and more. When the *Karina* crew changed watches at midnight, the wind had run all the way around the clock and was blowing a fresh 15 knots out of the east and northeast and the racers had "beautiful conditions" all the way to Bermuda.

In retrospect, the fleet had been clipped by a powerful low that passed to the east, a storm system reported to have a diameter of over 300 miles. It was a rough passage for many competitors, particularly those caught by the front while in the Stream. Some yachts reported 25-foot seas. John Pinheiro's *Fayal* from Dartmouth, Massachusetts lost her rudder and had to be towed by the USCG Cutter *Harriett Lane* over 200 miles into Bermuda.[50]

There were a few storms ashore as well. After each race the Compliance Committee meets in the elegant second floor conference room at RHADC where protests and compliance issues are discussed and addressed. Over forty years, Marion-Bermuda race organizers and officials have addressed many thorny issues, like pre-start collisions, missed marks, failed mandatory reporting and verification that sailors are, in

Orion, a Pearson 36, was chartered by Richard Carelton from her owner Bob Norton. Norton later signed on as navigator. *Orion* was the overall winner of the 1991 race. Photo: Jack Braitmayer

the Race Committee sufficient reason to exclude you from future Marion-Bermuda Races.

Yacht racing has been and continues to be a self-policing sport. Competitors are expected to abide by the rules, and to take the appropriate action (retirement, alternative penalty, or reporting the infringement) when they do not. Competitors who do not take the appropriate action are not welcome within the yacht racing community." [51]

Apart from the clear message on the importance of abiding by rules and the need for self-regulation in ocean racing, this letter and the investigative work behind it are evidence of a confident and well-run organization enforcing its rules with determination.

Kirk Cooper's 61' custom *Alphida* was first-to-finish in the 1991 race. In 1993, *Alphida* won on elapsed time again, breaking *War Baby's* course record by less than one minute, but on a shorter overall course. Photo: 1995 Marion-Bermuda Race Book

fact, Corinthian non-professionals. An example of how seriously the Compliance Committee takes the rules, and spirit, of the race, one competitor was overheard by another soliciting a weather report from a passing boat not involved in the race. The offending skipper made the mistake of not reporting the infraction upon his arrival in Bermuda. After researching the facts of the case, the race organizers found that they'd been misled. They then sent a letter banning the skipper from any future Marion-Bermuda races. They said:

"These actions, along with your behavior during the Compliance Committee hearing, have given

The 1993 Race

The 1993 race started in 20-knot headwinds and fog. The United States Naval Academy 44 *Swift* rammed Jeffrey Flower's *Growltiger* before the Class B start. Two midshipmen were injured, and both yachts withdrew. Once underway, it was a fast race. *SAIL* magazine reported that the 1993 race was "…the fastest Marion-Bermuda Race on record." The winners sailed a rhumb line course, and the Gulf Stream was benign.[52] Ron Noonan and *Wildflower* won on corrected time, exactly 10 years after their first win. He said: "It [the Gulf Stream] was a nonentity, since it ran perpendicular to the rhumb line." Bermudian and future RHADC Vice Commodore Buddy Rego won Class A honors on *Tsunami*, a Frers 41 and the smallest

Class A yacht. Rego told the *Royal Gazette*: "… the conditions the last few days were in our favor with the light air and us having a light boat…We [also] always had someone [we could see] to race against and this helped push us along."

Kirk Cooper in *Alphida* set a new Marion-Bermuda Race course record in 1993, besting *War Baby's* 1989 mark by a mere 21 seconds. To this day, however, fans of Warren Brown's *War Baby* maintain that *Alphida* didn't break the record. Their reasoning is that in 1993 the Bermuda finish line off St. David's lighthouse was changed from a line bearing 116 degrees magnetic from the lighthouse.[1] To the purist, the analysis goes like this: those 5 degrees of bearing shift amount to about 600 feet of distance (or one tenth of a nautical mile) if measured at positions 1 nautical mile off St. David's light, about where most boats cross. A big Marion-Bermuda race boat can sail at about 10 knots in a decent breeze. At that speed, she would cover 1 nautical mile every 6 minutes, or a

Damage to Jeffrey Flower's J40 *Growl Tiger* after being rammed prior to the Class B start in 1993. Photo: *SAIL*

The white block finish line tower (right) on the eastern end of Bermuda is adjacent to St. David's light. All Bermuda races use a finish line that extends from this tower. Officiating is by Bermudian volunteers. Photo: Fran Grenon

Dolly Pitcher (left) has been coordinating finish line provisioning for many Marion-Bermuda races. Tony Siese (right) is the voice of Bermuda Radio, and his "Welcome to Bermuda!" is among the most welcome sounds any Bermuda ocean racer will ever hear. Photo: Fran Grenon

Ed Rayner (left) enjoys the traditional finish line party with race Trustee and seven-time competitor Jack Braitmayer (center) and Trustee, competitor and former RHADC Commodore Charles Dunstan (right). Rayner coordinated Bermuda finish line operations for many years and retired after the 2015 Marion-Bermuda Race. Photo: Fran Grenon

tenth of a nautical mile every 36 seconds, neglecting current and leeway. So *Alphida* sailed a course that was 36 seconds shorter than *War Baby*, but she only beat *War Baby* time by 21 seconds! *Alphida* would have had to sail that last 0.1 miles at 36 knots to equal *War Baby*. She didn't.

Bermudian volunteers man the finish line for a major Bermuda races. Recently, chief among these is Eugene Rayner, who until his retirement after the 2013 race had participated or coordinated finish line operations for 30 years.[53] Tony Siese has handled radio operations, welcoming each racing yacht with "Welcome to Bermuda!," a very fine greeting after three or four days at sea in a small, and often very wet, boat. The finish line team includes four watch captains, radio operators, and "runners" who handle faxes and email reports of finishers and their times. A Bermudian named Dolly Pitcher has been responsible for refreshment deliveries to the finish line tower for many years. It is impossible to avoid noting the parallels between Bermuda's Dolly Pitcher and the folk-hero (and likely imaginary) American Molly Pitcher who carried water to refresh

Continental Army soldiers at the Revolutionary War battle of Monmouth, NJ, and allegedly took over artillery duties when her husband collapsed in battle.

Finish line duty demands much of the volunteers in the finish line tower adjacent to the St. David's lighthouse, and all Bermuda racers are grateful for their accuracy and service. They stand 24-hour watches while race fleets approach the island, and they don't leave the post unattended until every race boat has either finished the race or is accounted for and safe.

The 1995 Race

1995 was the tenth Marion-Bermuda Race. The fleet had a fast start but was becalmed in the Gulf Stream. On occasion, sailors becalmed in ocean races will take a swim. There's a certain amount of trust in doing so; in one's abilities as

Marion-Bermuda 1995
Cruising Yacht Race

Royal Hamilton Amateur Dinghy Club
Blue Water Sailing Club
Beverly Yacht Club

Carter Cordner and crew after their arrival at the RHADC in 1995. His Westsail 32 *Kemancha*, the smallest yacht in the fleet, won on corrected time. Photo: Charles Bascom

a swimmer, in those remaining aboard, and in the absence of predators from the deep. It's an odd feeling swimming in water more than a mile deep. But the refreshment an ocean swim brings often makes it worthwhile.

Dick Leather in *Columbine* was first to finish, and Carter Cordner in *Kemancha*, a Westsail 32 and the smallest boat in the fleet, won on corrected time. Cordner beat Ron Noonan in *Wildflower* by less than a half hour.

Service academy sailors are people of the highest stature and promise. The United States Naval Academy has sent two or more offshore yachts to compete in every Marion-Bermuda Race. The Academy's uniformed and disciplined officers and midshipmen are a fixture in Marion, and in Bermuda. In 1995, USNA 44 *Swift* returned to the course, and won Class B. The Navy sailors are exemplary competitors and often go on to great success in the military and in civilian life. Ensign Gary Huss from Kenosha, Wisconsin, skippered *Swift* in 1995. Ensign Bill Sena from Neptune Beach, Florida was his celestial navigator; the Naval Academy teams always use celestial navigation in Marion-

Bermuda. After his Class B win in the Marion-Bermuda Race, Huss earned his commission. His career literally "took off" from there. As reported in Aero-News:

"[Huss] reported to NAS Pensacola, FL, in 1996 to begin flight training. He earned his Wings of Gold in March 1999 at NAS Kingsville and was selected to fly the F-14 'Tomcat.' While assigned to the "Jolly Rogers" of Fighter Squadron (VF) 103, Huss completed two deployments to the Mediterranean Sea and Persian Gulf as part of Carrier Air Wing 17 embarked aboard USS George Washington (CVN-73). During these deployments, Huss flow contingency operations and combat air patrols enforcing the "No Fly Zone" over Southern Iraq in support of Operation Southern Watch, and on-call close air support operations over Afghanistan in support of Operation Enduring Freedom.

Huss returned to NAS Kingsville in 2003 as a flight instructor with VT-22. He left the active Navy component in 2006 and transferred directly into the Reserve component with the squadron. In addition to his new role as commanding officer of VT-22 Reserve, Huss serves as a first officer for United Airlines flying the Boeing 737 out of George H. W. Bush Intercontinental Airport in Houston."[54]

Race organizers, and host families on both the Marion and Bermuda ends of the race, have always welcomed Navy and Merchant Marine personnel to the events, including holding dinners and receptions in their honor. Marion resident Nancy McFadden and her late husband Dr. Samuel McFadden have for many years opened their home and hosted a reception for Navy and Merchant Marine sailors before each Marion-Bermuda race. One of their sons

The United States Naval Academy team sailed their Navy 44 *Swift* to a first-place finish in Class B in the 1995 race.
Photo: Charles Bascom

The Crealock 44 cutter *North Star* was sailed by G. Mike Rouzee to first place in Class D in the 1995 Marion-Bermuda Race.
Photo: Charles Bascom

attended the United States Naval Academy in Annapolis and competed in the race.

1995 was the first of three Class C wins for Alan Krulisch in his Cambria 40 *Crackerjack*. He would come back and do the same in 1997 and 1999, making *Crackerjack* on of the greats in Marion-Bermuda Race history.

The 1997 Race

The 1997 race was a "cruiser's race" according to *SAIL* magazine:

Marion-Bermuda 1997

Cruising Yacht Race

Royal Hamilton Amateur Dinghy Club
Blue Water Sailing Club
Beverly Yacht Club

"You could use GPS, but most preferred a sextant. You could have zigzagged between warm-and cold-water eddies, but this year most of the competitors in the Marion-Bermuda Race steered 165 degrees and had an easy time of it…This twentieth anniversary running of Marion-Bermuda was that rare and pleasant race when the moon was full and bright, the breeze never topped 20 knots, sea boots proved unnecessary, we never reefed (many boats never

Majek, a Tripp Javelin campaigned by Abbot Fletcher, won the 1997 race on corrected time. Photo: 1997 Marion-Bermuda Race Book

tacked), the Gulf Stream and its eddies were predictable, the weather held few surprises—what more was there to know!…This may be weather luck, but the Marion-Bermuda Race seems blessed by such harmony…While a 'cruising race' has something in common with being a little bit pregnant, Marion-Bermuda has evolved into an event that succeeds in providing the best of long-distance racing while minimizing performance and flat-out competition." [55]

First to finish went to Axel Rosenblad in *Akka*, a Palmer-Johnson 61 hailing from Atlantic Highlands, New Jersey. First overall was won by *Majek*, a 38-foot Tripp Javelin sloop sailed by Abbot Fletcher and his family from Bath, Maine.

This race was the first in which unlimited electronics were allowed, although most boats (70% of the fleet) and every trophy winner navigated celestially. In the 1995 race, electronics that measure things like depth, speed and wind were permitted, but direct position-finding equipment such as LORAN and GPS were prohibited except when yachts were close to land. In 1997, the organizers shifted their point of view. For the first time, GPS and LORAN were considered "standard," and those who chose to navigate using a sextant were awarded a 3%-time handicap bonus. The Marion-Bermuda Race organizers shifted from sticks to carrots; rather than penalize position-finding electronics, it rewarded celestial navigation. They have done so ever since.

The 1999 Race

1999 could be described as "The Year of the Swans." Richard Shulman was First-to-Finish in his Swan 51 *Temptress*. First Overall and First in Class B went to Doug

Ely in *Dakota*, a Swan 46. 1999 also was the first race when all-female crews competed, and one, *Caribe*, was a Swan 482.

The *Royal Gazette* reported on the new development:

"All-female crews will feature in this month's Marion-to-Bermuda Cruising Yacht race for the first time in the event's 22-year history…One of the race organizers, Faith Paulsen…felt the presence two all-women crews was encouraging. 'We've had boats skippered by women before, but never boats without a single man aboard…It's great to see it happening and I think they're very courageous.'" The two boats were *Caribe,* skippered by Anne Chapin and *Chautaqua*, campaigned by Pamela Westrom." [56]

By the 2005 race, the organizers recognized the importance of recognizing all-women yachts by awarding a special trophy. In honor of her commitment to women in competitive sailing, both as the first woman Commodore of the Beverly Yacht Club and her encouragement of women in racing, the organizers named the special prize the "Faith Paulsen Trophy."

The 1999 race also was the first Marion-Bermuda Race in which the organizers separated the fleet into an Electronic class, and a Celestial class. Of the 103 yachts that started the race, 55 yachts elected celestial, and 48 electronic. Many returning competitors, including such Marion-Bermuda successes as *War Baby, Wildflower, Bermuda Oyster* and *Majek* were still navigated by sextant, but the electronic class was growing. In 1997, 75% of the fleet raced with the celestial designation. In 1999 it was 53%. By 2001, the percentage had declined to 31%. The most recent races have had 25-30% of the fleet race under

Marion-Bermuda 1999
Cruising Yacht Race

Royal Hamilton Amateur Dinghy Club
Blue Water Sailing Club
Beverly Yacht Club

the celestial navigation bonus.

Marion-Bermuda Race organizers continue to examine and debate the virtues and limitations between electronic and celestial navigation. On the one hand, celestial navigation is consistent with and supportive of the ethos of the Marion-Bermuda Race. A sailor who can accurately establish a position at sea using good sextant, sight reduction and plotting technique, and use that information to get from New England to Bermuda safely and fast, is held in high regard by the Marion-Bermuda Race organizers. On the one hand, Global Positioning System (GPS) technologies give a yacht at sea accurate, inexpensive, and virtually real-time position information. Derivative systems such as Digital Selective Calling (DSC), instant man overboard position-plotting on chart plotters, and Automatic Information Systems (AIS) that send and receive position and course information to other yachts and ships in the area can be vital safety tools. On the other hand, competence in celestial position-finding is a safety tool as well. If a yacht experiences a catastrophic power failure (which several have in the long history of the race), electronic navigation equipment may become useless. Careful sailors may ship handheld or independent battery-operated equipment, but cost can be an issue as well.

Prior to every Marion-Bermuda Race the organizers reexamine these of trade-offs. To date, they have kept a celestial navigation class. All yachts carry GPS-based equipment for safety reasons, but the positional information displayed by those devices is carefully placarded so that these sailors steer to Bermuda using only their compass, and the sun, moon, stars.

Celestial Navigation

As of this writing, the Marion-Bermuda Race is the only major ocean race offering a trophy for the first-to-finish celestially-navigated yacht on corrected time. Throughout its history, how well and by what method a yacht is navigated has been considered as important as every other element in sailing yacht ocean racing—yacht and crew preparation, sail selection and trim, Buzzards Bay tactics, Gulf Stream and weather routing, and the many other factors that combine for success. In fact, given the more than forty years the Marion-Bermuda Race has run, how the race organizers have chosen to address celestial composes a history of the transition of recreational navigation from predominantly celestial to overwhelmingly electronic.

Celestial navigation is the ancient art and science of using the sun, moon and stars to find one's position in a largely featureless space like a desert, tundra, or ocean. The earliest systematic oceanic celestial navigators generally are recognized to be the Phoenicians (fl. 1000-300 B.C.E.), who sailed great distances across the Mediterranean Sea and into the Atlantic and Indian Oceans out of sight of land. They had observed that the movement of celestial objects was repetitive, and therefore predictable. This gave rise to the earliest astronomers and celestial observers - the astrologers. By knowing this regularity, astrologers could "see into the future." They also noted that the sky looked differently in different locations, and that those differences also were predictable. The Europeans belatedly picked up on the idea. Portugal's Prince Henry the Navigator (fl. 1430-1460 C.E.) determined that his nation's future depended upon the development of a new trade route to Asia that bypassed the profit-hungry middlemen of Venice and Arabia, so he

Ron Wisner, winner of the 2013 celestial navigation trophy, now instructs sailors on the finer points of celestial navigation.
Photo: Georgia Sparling, sippicanvillagesoup.com

sent astrologers to sea to observe and record the change in celestial object position as the ship's position changed. It was a brilliant feat of astrological reverse-engineering and produced the earliest examples of predictive celestial navigation tables developed at sea.

Regularity, predictability and uniqueness depending on location—the foundations of a position-finding system. These fundamentals of oceanic celestial navigation haven't changed. What have evolved since the Phoenicians, Arabs and Prince Henry are navigation table comprehensiveness and accuracy, and the instruments used at sea to measure angles and time. The last 500 years of celestial navigation has been about improvements in angular measurement, time keeping, and tables.

Electronic navigation methods were, of course, available to the sailors in the first Marion-Bermuda races. Radio Direction Finding (RDF) had been widely used in yachting for decades, but only for relatively short range heading confirmation. After World War II, LORAN (Long Range Navigation) technology was built out by the government and became available to non-military users. However, it wasn't until the mid-1970s that microelectronics had developed to a point where LORAN-C technology met the usefulness criteria for sailors at sea: small size, low power consumption, and reasonable price. At that point, the pressure increased for logical sailors to convert from celestial to electronic navigation techniques. But not all sailors are logical.

The first several Marion-Bermuda races assumed that celestial navigation was central because competence in it was evidence of competence in seamanship. In addition, the post-war sailing world was full of military-trained celestial navigators. Dickie Bird was one. What eventually differentiated Marion-Bermuda was the recognition by its founders and early race organizers that the advance of electronics, initially LORAN and its surface-based variants, and then eventually GPS and its satellite-based variants, threatened the art and science of celestial navigation and what they viewed to be the soul of offshore seamanship. They also felt it might be a safety issue. As typically conservative seamen, the founders never fully trusted electronics. In a 1995 interview with the *Royal Gazette* Dickie Bird said:

> "I think that what we've always stressed is that people should be competent navigators, that on each boat there should be a competent navigator, a celestial navigator...somebody who can actually take his sights and produce his position on a chart...We still feel there ought to be one race where celestial navigation is required because we think it's essential. It's all very well to say electronics will do everything, but it won't do everything."

In 1977, the Marion-Bermuda Notice of Race (NOR) said the following about navigation allowances and limitations:

> 1.6 *Electronic Gear.* Depth finders and RDF may be used at any time. Loran, Omega, radar and similar electronic equipment may be used within the 20 fathom depth contour of the departure coast and again when estimated to be within 50 miles of Bermuda. By acceptance of a 5% penalty on the handicap rating, electronic navigation equipment may be used *at any time*. In either case, a navigator skilled in and equipped for celestial navigation must be aboard.

In fact, the handicap penalty on the unlimited use of electronic position-finding equipment at sea was increased from 5% to 8%.

With the advent of reliable and affordable GPS systems in the 1990s, the tide finally turned in attitudes toward celestial navigation and its place in the spirit of the Marion-Bermuda Race. Celestial has evolved from a necessity, into a back-up system in the context of new and unreliable electronics, and finally into an element of accomplished seamanship that should be recognized, encouraged, and rewarded. In 1995 the Marion-Bermuda Race became an event that encouraged celestial navigation instead of penalized electronics, and in 2001 celestial navigators were put into a race class of their own. Today, a yacht navigated celestially in the open ocean between 50 miles of either coast is awarded a 3% rating bonus.

Brad Curtis in his Passport 40 *Cricket* is the stand-on vessel during the confused Class E start of the 2007 Marion-Bermuda Race. Photo: Fran Grenon

The 2000s: From Record Calm to Record Rough

The Marion-Bermuda Race has been adaptable. In the 1970s, the founders and organizers adapted to the professionalism trends in sailing, and in sports in general, by creating a sustainable Corinthian ocean race, encouraging amateurs and families to test their mettle as blue water sailors. In the 1990s, the organizers adapted to developments in navigation methods by initially penalizing boats that chose electronic position-finding methods, but then evolving to accept electronics as standard, and rewarding celestial navigation with a time bonus. In the late 1990s all-women boats were welcomed and eventually a special trophy was established for all-female competitors. In the 2000s, as competitive sailing went through a diminution of interest due to recession and distraction, Marion-Bermuda Race organizers established new trophies and classes to attract as many competitors as possible to their biennial event. These included yachts that competed in multiple races like the Newport to Bermuda, Marblehead to Halifax, and Marion-Bermuda races, as well as trying out classes for multi-hulls and classic yachts. It's likely that these adaptations and innovations will continue as Corinthian sailing and ocean racing evolve.

The RHADC is the epicenter of the social and trophy award events in Bermuda following each Marion-Bermuda Race. For example, a fashion show followed the 2013 race. Photo: Fran Grenon

The 2001 Race

The 2001 race holds the distinction of being the slowest Marion-Bermuda Race on record. In some races, not much happens, and this was one of those races. The start was orderly and largely uneventful in a pleasant southeasterly. Buzzards Bay was well behaved, as was the Gulf Stream, but the fleet ran out of wind in the Atlantic. *Veritas*, a light-displacement Frers 46 sailed by Philip Hutchinson was first to finish. The trip took five and one half days, a plodding passage record that still stands. The becalmed fleet was bunched and slow, and after everyone had finally arrived, *Veritas* had fallen to 22nd on corrected time. First overall went to James Lawless aboard *Spinache*, a celestially-navigated Island Packet 35,

and not surprisingly, painted green. *Solace*, skippered by David Owen, won on corrected time in the electronic navigation class.

The RHADC and Bermuda welcome Marion-Bermuda sailors with dinners, cocktail parties, awards ceremonies and special events. One of those events since has been a "friends and family" racing events held in the Great Sound after the ocean race is done, skippers and crews are well-rested, but many are eager to get back onto the water. Family members and friends who did not race to Bermuda but have flown in to enjoy the post-race celebrations often enjoy getting a taste of closed-course sailing as well. These events followed the 2001 race with more than 50 boats participating.

US Army Captain (Ret.) Guy Jones (second from left) sailed his Pacific Seacraft 40 cutter *Gorgeous Girl* to first overall in the 2003 race. Photo: Guy Jones

The 2003 Race

The 2003 race was won by Guy Jones in *Gorgeous Girl*, a 40-foot Pacific Seacraft cutter. Jones served in Vietnam from 1966 to 1969. US Army captain Jones was a helicopter pilot, and when his helicopter was shot down he was wounded, resulting in the loss of his right hand. Revealing a marvelous sense of humor lurking just under a refined intellect, he once said in an interview that his limitation gives deeper meaning to the idea of "short-handed sailing."

When interviewed for this writing, and in news reports published after the *Gorgeous Girl* win, Jones talked about how he approached the race analytically. He studied weather patterns, Gulf Stream behaviors, past race winner routes and tactics, and the facts of his own boat. Long before it was common, he built a computer model of exactly how *Gorgeous Girl* would and should be sailed, and what their results would be.

Roy Greenwald posted a reminder to his crew aboard *Cordelia* to remain vigilant throughout the 2003 race. The reminder paid off; *Cordelia* won first overall among celestial boats. Photo: Roy Greenwald

His model indicated that *Gorgeous Girl* should arrive in Bermuda in 96 hours, or in exactly 4 days. Instead, she arrived 6 hours late, in 4 days and 6 hours, and Jones was somewhat disappointed, not in their performance, but by his own forecast. He was a little annoyed that it hadn't been more accurate. As it turned out, once all competitors had finished and handicaps applied, *Gorgeous Girl* won her class and the race overall. Unpredictable nature had intervened and slowed the entire fleet. First-time competitor and one-handed sailor Guy Jones had won, a very satisfying victory for the entire Marion-Bermuda Race enterprise.

Starr Trail was sailed by Robert Mulderig and an Anglo-Bermudian crew. This was at least the second Mulderig yacht named for the famously steep and fast ski run on Mt. Mansfield in Stowe, Vermont. They were first to finish and winners of Class A1, the celestial group for larger boats. *Starr Trail* came to within an hour of beating Bermudian Kirk Cooper's short course record set in 1993 with *Alphida*.

Since 2001, the organizers had segmented the fleet into yachts using unlimited electronic position-finding equipment, and those using celestial methods, and Mulderig chose celestial. *Cordelia* won the celestial class on corrected time. The Valiant 42 was commanded by the husband/wife team of Roy and Gail Greenwald. Gail navigated and won the Navigator's Trophy for guiding her yacht to the celestial win.

Bermuda yachts had great success in the 2003 race. *Starr Trail* was first to finish. *Bermuda Oyster*, an Oyster 435 sailed by perennial competitor Paul Hubbard with an Anglo-Bermuda crew (including Neil Redburn who later would become Commodore of RHADC) is a Bermuda-based boat with a Beverly Yacht Club-member skipper, and *Bermuda Oyster* won the Bermuda Longtail Trophy for the best performance by a BYC yacht. And finally, *Lullaby*, a Starratt 45 skippered by David Roblin of Southampton won the Bavier Trophy for exemplary seamanship. Just before the starting gun, an engine room electrical fire broke out aboard *Lullaby*. The fire eliminated all electronics. The crew brought the conflagration under control, and over the next several days at sea rewired the main circuits to restore power. Later in the race their starter motor, as well as a backup motor, burned out. Despite their misadventures with electricity, *Lullaby* won Class C and was the first Bermuda boat to finish on corrected time.

Panama Red, a Beneteau First 42 and veteran of previous races, including a First-in-Class B in 1993, was skippered by Rebecca Bioty and finished strong with her all-women crew and was awarded the first Faith Paulsen trophy. In an article in the 2007 race book, Bioty said:

> "Once underway, sailing with women is significantly different from sailing with men. I've raced with both and can say this from experience. Women are kinder, more caring, and far better nurses to the sick, ailing or injured. If a crew member is feeling low and tired, women are more than willing to stand an extra watch. They sing and tell stories long into the dark nights to keep each other entertained. They are

Corinthian Resolve: The Story of the Marion-Bermuda Race

mothers, nurses, wives and friends. And when the race is over, they hug, cry, laugh and smile at the stories and experiences they have all shared." [57]

This may be true, but gender doesn't in any way hinder competitiveness and a good sea-sense. The author's daughter has sailed in three Marion-Bermuda races; two on a mixed gender boat, and one in 2015 aboard *Etoile,* a Stellar 52 that hails from Tiverton, RI. *Etoile* is owned and skippered by Anne Kolker. Kolker and core members of her

crew have competed as an all-women boat in three Marion-Bermuda Races. Lisa Gabrielson McCurdy wrote:

"In the 2015 Race, I sailed with Anne through the remnants of low-pressure system where we saw steady seas at 12-15 feet, and wind gusting into the low 40's. We sailed under 1/3 main and 1/3 of the jib for more than 35 hours, making our way carefully through the Gulf Stream and closer to Bermuda. Save for a few of the crew, these were the

81

The 2000s: From Record Calm to Record Rough

The all women crew aboard *Etoile* after the 2015 race. Anne Kolker and her crews have been consistent winners of the Faith Paulsen trophy awarded to first overall finisher among all women yachts. Photo: Fran Grenon

wildest conditions we had ever seen, but Anne knew her boat and knew exactly what *Etoile* and her crew could handle. We made it to Bermuda without incident in the fastest finish of my three experiences."[58]

Any sailor would enjoy being aboard a yacht with the camaraderie and spirit of a *Panama Red*, but the all-women Marion-Bermuda boats also are raced to win.

The 2005 Race

In 2005, Marion-Bermuda added satellite tracking as a safety feature, and a new method to give real-time progress reporting to folks on shore. In addition, a multi-hull class for cata-

marans and trimarans was added, another good example of the organizers innovating in response to sailing trends. Multi-hulls had been gaining popularity, particularly as charter yachts in warm climates. The Marion-Bermuda Race has been an inclusive race, and multi-hull sailors who were cruising-oriented and ocean competent were welcomed. There were seven entries on the scratch sheet, and five finished what turned out to be a relatively slow race in light air. Despite the conditions, heart surgeon Lars Svensson crossed the finish line in his Open 60 trimaran *Heartsease Laurus Roc* approximately 12 hours ahead of the next finisher. This despite having started in Buzzards Bay 24 hours after the monohulls, and recovering a man overboard enroute. *Heartsease* had to use her engine to retrieve the wet sailor.

The 2005 race was the first to feature a multi-hull class. Photo: Fran Grenon

John Carey, Compliance Committee Chairman for that race, wrote to Svensson after the finish saying that because the engine start was an "…action taken solely for the safe recovery of a crew member washed overboard while making emergency repairs…" *Heartsease* would not be penalized.[59] Multihulls and monohulls did not compete head-to-head, being separated by class and subject to entirely different handicapping schemes. After the initial success in 2005, multi-hulls competed again in 2007 and 2009, but then interest faded. Ray Cullum, a long-time race organizer and Director of Marketing for Marion-Bermuda, said that the

practice ended after three races probably due to declining involvement in ocean racing within the New England multi-hull sailing community.[60]

The passage had been in relatively light air and a well-behaved Gulf Stream. Robert Mulderig said to the *Royal Gazette* that a high-pressure system dominated the race-course and so the wind was expected to be light. He was correct. He and *Starr Trail* withdrew from the race along with 25 other entries due to the slow conditions. Thomas Bock and his US Naval Academy crew aboard the N/M 49 *Mameluke* crossed the line first in four days, five hours and

The 2000s: From Record Calm to Record Rough

ABOVE: Christopher Streit's black Bermuda 40
Fandango (left) leads the Class E fleet at the start
of the 2005 race. He is chased by (left to right)
Glen Urban in *Chickadee III*, David Caso in *Silhouette*
and Mark Nunes in *Windflower II*.
Photo: Fran Grenon

RIGHT: A tale of two Hinckleys: The white Pilot 35
and eventual overall winner *Panacea* (left) and the
black-hulled Bermuda 40 *Fandango* cross the starting
line between the committee boat and Gong 1 in
Buzzards Bay in the 2005 race.
Photo: Fran Grenon

Mameluke maneuvering astern of James Feeney's yawl *Kathleen* (US 83).
The US Naval Academy team sailed the red N/M 49 to a first-to-finish in 2005 and used celestial navigation.
Photo: Fran Grenon

The 2000s: From Record Calm to Record Rough

David Caso and *Silhouette*, a Cherubini 44 racing in Class D, won the 2007 race on corrected time. Photo: Fran Grenon

Preston Hutchins sailing *Morgan's Ghost,* a Swan NYYC 42, to first-to-finish in 2007. Photo: Fran Grenon

58 minutes, nearly one day slower than the *Alphida* record set in 1993. Gus McDonald from the Harraseeket Yacht Club in South Freeport, Maine won the overall trophy in *Panacea*, a Hinckley Pilot 35.

Panacea was one of 13 yachts hailing from Maine that year. George Denny in his custom Alden 45 *Restive* built at Brooklin Boat Yard in Maine won the celestial class. Denny and his crew would have an exciting return from Bermuda in heavy weather in 2015.

The United States Naval Academy has sent boats to compete in the Marion-Bermuda Race since its inception in 1977. The Massachusetts Maritime Academy also has had a competitor in Marion-Bermuda since 2005. With their well-disciplined crews and competently handled boats, the service academies are always impressive sights on Buzzards Bay and in Hamilton harbor. Navy boats always are navigated celestially, and often win trophies, both within their own class of service academies, but also as direct competitors with the civilian yachts in the race. As mentioned above, the Navy boat *Mameluke* was first to finish in 2005. The Massachusetts Maritime Academy won that honor in 2015 in *Mischievous*.

The 2007 Race

Seventy-three yachts turned out in 2007, the 30th anni-versary of the race. Like 2005, the fleet had a relatively slow and uneventful passage to Bermuda. The Cherubini 44 *Silhouette* won on corrected time, the first of seven trophies won by David Caso and his crew, including three first-in-class wins. Preston Hutchins in *Morgan's Ghost*, a white-hulled NYYC Swan 44, was first across the line.

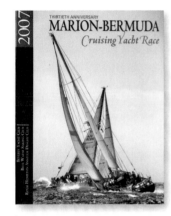

Each year, the organizers publish a race book that contains the Notice of Race, Sailing Instructions, guides to Marion and Bermuda, descriptions and latest news from the three sponsoring clubs, and often an article or two about topics of interest. The race book published for the 2009 race was coordinated and written by Bill Kennedy and Bob Hlady. One, or both, of them interviewed a number of 2007 competitors, as well as several veterans of prior races, to determine exactly why people raced in Marion-Bermuda.[61] John Elliott, skipper of *Yukon Jack* and overall winner in 1989, said it was for the "adventure," citing the time when the boat was in a "…deep trough … in 1989 when he glanced up at the adjacent swell. Riding near the crest, a humpback whale and her calf were looking down into his cockpit." In another interview, Kennedy and Hlady heard Buddy Rego, a Commodore of RHADC and the 1993 Class A winner in *Tsunami* say: "For the first six hours of the [foggy start of the] race, to hear crashing

sails and boats tacking all around you, without ever seeing them, is a very daunting experience. It was almost surreal." Sam Vineyard who skippered his J-46 *Hawke* to a near first-to-finish in 2005, said about his fast passage across the Gulf Stream in strong wind and a beam reach: "You get one of those kinds of days [once every] ten years, and you'll keep coming back for it for the rest of your life." Paul Rasmussen, a veteran of ten Marion-Bermuda races, it's the destination that matters, and the people he arrives there with. He said: "I have never stepped off the boat disliking somebody." Samuel Gray talked about the simplicity of ocean sailing: "Getting from point A to point B is all there is, and there's nothing else." The author(s) conclude the article with:

> "Or maybe few words are best. As Buddy Rego said, the appeal is in the tactics, the disconnection from the rest of the world, the solitude, the accomplishment and camaraderie. 'I don't think you need any more than that.'"

The 2009 Race

The 2009 race was a great one, but the finish line belonged to one boat. Martin Jacobson sailed his British Virgin Islands-registered Swan 44 Mk II *Crescendo* to First-to-Finish, First Overall, and First in Celestial. Not since *Gabriella* in 1979 (following *Silkie* in 1977) had a yacht won the

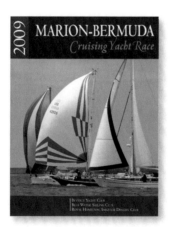

race on both elapsed and corrected times. *Crescendo* also won First in Class, was a co-winner of the team trophy, and Jacobson's celestial navigator Jeremy Whitty won the Navigator's Trophy.

Martin Jacobson's crew drives *Crescendo* across the line for an exciting Class B start in 2009.
Crescendo finished first on elapsed and corrected time and used celestial navigation. Photo: Fran Grenon

The passage wasn't particularly fast, but the boats and crews worked hard to get to Bermuda safely. Jacobson crossed the line off St. David's in 4 days, 15 hours and 32 minutes, finishing in the dim early light of an overcast and blowy Bermuda morning. She crossed two hours ahead of Chris Culver's powerful Hinckley 59 *Cetacea*, but on corrected time finished nearly 14 hours ahead of his nearest competitor, *Defiance*, a Navy 44 skippered by Robert King.

The 2009 race will be remembered for the big winds and large waves for the entire race. A frontal system with a large pressure-gradient moved slowly across the racecourse. The winds had predominantly a southerly component, favoring the bigger boats, and those with windward ability. For them, it was hard work. For smaller boats, and for those rigged to reach, 2009 was a windward slog. Of 46 starters, only 26 finished the race. But only a handful didn't at least give it a try; most who retired from the race did so once they were at sea and could witness first-hand the difficult conditions. Ron Wisner, skipper of the classic Rhodes 41 yawl *Hotspur* and an experienced blue water sailor and celestial navigator, wrote the following for the 2011 race book:

"The day of the race was windy and wet, and…I had the feeling we were already in the early stages of the dreadful forecast we got at Skippers Meeting… By nightfall [Saturday], the wind was in the mid-teens…*Hotspur* came alive on a close reach…The thrill of flying on a close reach was short-lived. With the wind building *Hotspur* was soon over powered and we reduced to the blade [jib]. As the wind spiked to twenty-five knots we dropped the main going on blade and mizzen. The wind was now blowing thirty knots. Suddenly…the mizzen sheet broke. Sure enough, it was the only rigging I had not replaced. As the wind continued to escalate, we quickly dropped the mizzen and lashed the boom to the mizzen shroud so it would not cause more damage.

None of us had really slept since the race [had] started and morning comes early near the summer solstice. With the wind in the high thirties and increasing we prepared to set the storm jib. After dropping the blade I crawled to the foredeck on hands and knees to hank on the jib that we never really expected to need. That day we saw 45 knots of apparent wind while on a quartering tack doing four to five knots. The [true] wind must have been close to fifty knots.

The next few days were rainy and windy but nothing like before. There is nothing to compare with the camaraderie of six people in a small boat in a storm in the North Atlantic…we didn't care that we arrived dead last." [62]

The winds recorded by competitors in 2009 are among the highest ever reported for the Marion-Bermuda Race. Like fishermen, ocean sailors can exaggerate conditions, and wave heights are particularly difficult to estimate from the cockpit of a small boat. Large waves look huge, and huge waves seem enormous. However, wind speeds are different—digital anemometers are difficult to argue with. Boats in the 2009 race reported peak gusts as high as 50 knots. The 1979 race also was rough, but there are no surviving reports of 50 knots like the breeze experienced in 2009. This makes Martin Jacobson's triple-win in *Crescendo* even more noteworthy.

Bermuda fitted dinghys underway downwind. Photo: Neil Redburn

Bermuda Fitted Dinghy

A Bermuda fitted dinghy is a small open dingy "fitted" with a lightly ballasted keel and enormous sails. They initially were sailing adaptations of rowing boats used by native fishermen, pilots and ferrymen. Keels were "fitted" to these sailing rowboats in the nineteenth century to allow them to carry their extreme sail plan.

Stem to stern the hull measures just over 14'. They have a 5' beam and 18" draft absent the fitted "fan" keel which adds 3' to the draft. Where it gets interesting is in the spar and sail plans. On this 14' hull Bermudians rig a 14' bowsprit,

a 24' boom, and a 38' mast. The mainsail is loose-footed and droops below the boom. The boat carries a jib and a spinnaker. Technical specifications published in *Rudder* magazine in 1906 tersely said that the center of gravity for these boats is "up the mast." These days six adults are needed to keep them upright in a breeze. An historical monograph in the RHADC archives said that the Bermuda fitted dinghy is a "crazy little boat."

A plaque in the bar at the RHADC tells the early history of the Bermuda fitted dinghy and how it and Dinghy Club origins are intertwined:

The first use of the word 'dinghey' referring to a small boat, appears in the *Royal Gazette* in 1843. The first recorded 'dinghey' race in Bermuda was held in July, 1853 in St. George's harbor, restricted to one-masted open boats not over 12 feet [overall]. Five years later races were organized in Hamilton harbor by members of the Bermuda Native Yacht Club with professional crews. The participation of amateurs led to the formation of the Hamilton Amateur Dinghey Association in 1882. Short of the interruptions caused by world wars, 'dinghy' racing has continued ever since. This sport is part of our Bermuda heritage...[63]

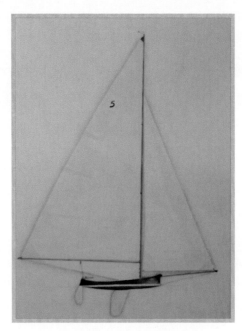

A drawing on the wall at RHADC shows the hull form and extreme sail plan of a Bermuda fitted dinghy. Photo by the Author

ballast and crew are aboard when the spar is put in.

Each dinghy is provided with three suits of leg-of-mutton sails, one for light weather, another for moderate breezes, the third for a heavy wind. Consequently, when the boats are being made ready for a race, their crews dress them in accordance with the weather prospects, and it some-times is necessary to change sails between events...

Each boat carries four men and a boy—all amateur sailors. The latter's work is to bail, for the boats are not decked, and frequently sail with their gunwales under water. The chief member of the crew is the 'conner' who sits opposite the mast, tends the jib sheets and watches every move of his antagonists. Next to him is the man who handles the shifting ballast, then the one who holds the mainsheets, and finally the helmsman. The boy sits in the bottom and bails continually, but, if the wind softens, and it is neces-sary to lighten the boat, he jumps overboard, trusting to some friendly spectator to pick him up".[64]

Neil Redburn, an RHADC Commodore and keen fitted dinghy racer and believer, described dinghy racing during an interview in Bermuda. The impression he conveyed is that a Bermuda fitted dinghy race is analogous to a good-natured amateur rugby match, only instead of on a grass pitch, it takes place on the water. The mood is light before the start and after the finish, but while the competition is underway, jaws are set, eyes narrowed, and the rules are constantly interpreted and perhaps re-interpreted. Libations flow liberally, particularly during the after-race celebrations, perhaps in part motivated by everyone involved thanking providence that they haven't been drowned. Things haven't changed much over the years.

In 1914, the *Royal Gazette* described dinghy preparation in those days:

"First the mast is stepped, and, a dinghy despite its deep keel is so cranky that she will capsize unless

The Bermuda fitted dinghy is testament to Bermudian sailing culture. It's unique to the island, offers enjoyable (albeit usually wet) competition, and has 175 years of history behind it. Above all, it was created and perfected by amateur sailors. There are four fitted dinghies actively racing in Bermuda waters now and three are in storage. We hope that the class enjoys continued popularity and many more seasons of success.

A Bermuda fitted dinghy can be an exhilarating ride.
Photo: Neil Redburn

BELOW: Fortunately the water in Bermuda is a pleasant temperature. Fitted dinghys capsize easily, but the swim can be refreshing on a hot day.
Photo: Neil Redburn

The 2000s: From Record Calm to Record Rough

The custom 72' yawl *Kathleen* rail down at the start of the Marion-Bermuda Race in Buzzards Bay. Photo: Fran Grenon

![Chapter 7]

Marion-Bermuda in Its Fifth Decade

The Marion-Bermuda Race entered its fifth decade in 2011. Like all ocean races, participation dropped off due to the Great Recession of 2008-2010, but never dropped below levels where the race would be economically viable and competitively interesting. The three sponsoring clubs remained fully engaged and committed, and although some classes like multihulls were dropped, others, like classic and sail-training yachts, were added. A big-boat class was added in 2011, creating a separate class for boats with overall lengths from 60 to 100 feet. This was to recognize that vessels significantly larger than those typically seen in the Marion-Bermuda Race were, and will in the future be, raced with their owners in command and all-amateur crews aboard.

The 2011 Race

One of those larger boats came to the starting line in 2011. *Lilla* is a red Briand-designed 76 cutter registered in Ireland. The boat is owned by Simon De Pietro. His wife, Nancy, is among the race crew. The 2011 race began in Buzzards Bay with 49 yachts at the line, including one owned and raced by this author—it was our first ocean race. The wind was a strong sou'wester, reaching 20 knots sustained. Being in class C, one of the slower classes, we started about 30 minutes ahead of *Lilla*. By
the time we'd tacked to the Sow and Pigs bell at the entrance to the Bay, *Lilla* had passed us, the rest of the fleet and was on her way to a record-smashing passage to Bermuda.

Two minutes to the start
aboard *Lilla*, the Briand 76
cutter sailed by Simon and
Nancy De Pietro to an elapsed
time record in the 2011 race.
Photo: Nancy De Pietro

As is sometimes the case in the Marion-Bermuda Race, a weather pattern like the frontal passage we had in 2011, will create, in effect, two races. In 2011, most of the fleet was behind the front, and in fact, many ran into a dead calm "wind hole" south of the Gulf Stream. This cost us at least 12 hours. In addition, after the frontal passage, the Bermuda high settled back in over our destination, and as we and many other competitors approached Bermuda, the fleet literally ran out of wind. We and nine other boats were forced to retire from the race due to a lack of wind and motor in to Hamilton.

Lilla didn't suffer that fate. She got away fast, stayed west of the rhumb line, and rode the frontal system all the way to Bermuda. She arrived in 2 days, 20 hours, 58 minutes and 45 seconds, smashing the elapsed time record set by *Alphida* in 1993 by nearly 10 hours. Nancy De Pietro wrote in an article published in the 2013 race book: "We were early. We attended the race committee [finish line] party at St. David's Light House and had the pleasure of watching the second yacht finish as we sipped Dark-n-Stormys on the hill." [65] Sean Saslo in *Brigand* crossed the finish line 7 hours and 30 minutes after *Lilla*, also besting *Alphida's* course record.

Race conditions were perfect for a big cutter like *Lilla* and she was well-sailed to a First-to-Finish and a First Overall, a feat accomplished only by *Silkie* (1977), *Gabriella* (1979) and *Crescendo* (2009). Among other prizes, *Lilla* also won the Bermuda Ocean Cruising Yacht Trophy, a highly prestigious trophy awarded to a yacht that races well in both the Marion-Bermuda Race and the Newport to Bermuda race in its cruising class. In 2010, the De Pietros and *Lilla* took fifth in their cruising class in the Newport to Bermuda race.

Sail training vessel *Spirit of Bermuda* made her first appearance in the Marion-Bermuda Race in 2011. The vessel was one of the last designs by marine architect Bill

Lilla crossing the finish line under reefed main and staysail off St. David's light while setting a new course record and posting an overall win in the 2011 Marion-Bermuda Race.
Photo: Fran Grenon

Langan. Her design was inspired by the Bermuda sloop, a fast merchant and trading vessel built in Bermuda, usually of Bermuda cedar, in the eighteenth and nineteenth centuries. *Spirit* is wood, 86' on deck, and 112' sparred. *Spirit* is a three-masted "Ballyhoo" Bermuda schooner with loose-footed Marconi foresail, main and boomed spanker. She was built at Rockport Marine in Maine, and launched in the summer of 2006. On her tenth birthday, she was treated to a several-months refit at Rockport.

She is Bermuda's national "tall ship," representing the island and its maritime heritage. *Spirit* is owned and operated by the Bermuda Sloop Foundation. This organization was founded by three Bermuda philanthropists who saw the need for: "... programs for character and education development through experiential learning." [66] In the 2011

Spirit of Bermuda is a Maine-built replica of a Bermuda sloop. She is Bermuda's national "tall ship" and youth sea training vessel for the nation. Photo: Fran Grenon

race, and when she returned for another go in 2013, she carried a group of Bermudian youth who had the time of their lives sailing the powerful and graceful schooner 645 miles from Marion to Bermuda. Bermuda's Governor His Excellency George Fergusson sailed aboard *Spirit* in the 2013 race, and reported in a post-race interview that he had an enjoyable time and were he to remain in Bermuda, he would have "done it again!" Fergusson has returned to the UK in the normal course of succession, and the organizers hope that future Bermuda Governors will be as interested in the Marion-Bermuda Race as George Fergusson, whether aboard *Spirit* or with another competitor.

Corinthian Resolve: The Story of the Marion-Bermuda Race

The 2013 Race

In 2013, and again in 2015, the Massachusetts Maritime Academy entered dominant boats. *Shindig* is an Andrew 68. Equipped with coffee-grinder winches and a 7' diameter wheel, the boat was sailed by 12 amateurs, primarily cadets with only limited big boat sailing experience. But the boat

was fast. In an article in the 2015 race book, MMA sailing master Chuck Fontaine said that training the crew was a major emphasis during the short spring before the June 19, 2013 start. They trained hard, including competing in the traditional Figawi Race in May.

The 2013 start was downwind in a fresh 20-knots of cool air out of the northwest. Most boats crossed the starting line at near hull speed under reefed main and full genoa. A few tried their asymmetrical spinnaker, but the result was increased complexity and risk with little added speed. In our case, we had difficulty snuffing the chute when wind gusts exceeded 25 knots and the boat labored under too much sail. This writer and one watch captain suffered severe hand burns when a halyard and a snuffer line got away. The sail was eventually brought under control but at some cost to position in the race.

Shindig, on the other hand, roared out of the bay under poled symmetrical chute. Fontaine said that they covered 521 miles in 48 hours, an average speed of nearly 11 knots over the bottom. But then *Shindig* ran into the Bermuda high. "…*Shindig* stopped dead in her tracks. We went from 24 knots in Buzzards Bay to 17 knots in the Sargasso Sea to 0 knots east of the Gulf Stream…Our frustration grew along with the concern that we would be passed by those behind us on the wings of a fresh breeze we would be the last to see." [67] The fact is that conditions did cause

Shindig, an Andrew 68 sailed by Massachusetts Maritime Academy cadets, departing Buzzards Bay at near hull speed under spinnaker in the 2013 race. *Shindig* was first to finish. Photo: Fran Grenon

a bunching of the fleet as the *Shindig* crew feared. They won first overall with a time of 3 days, 14 hours and 40 minutes, a very respectable time. On corrected time, Ian Gumprecht in *Roust*, a Sea Sprite 34, won the overall trophy. Gumprecht also won Class C, first double-handed boat (with crewmate Mark Swanson). Their accomplishment was significant, and celebrated at their home club. Gumprecht reported later:

"On our return home to Oyster Bay we were greeted by a flotilla of Flag Officers from Seawanhaka Corinthian Yacht Club who passed us a bottle of champagne. They then escorted us to the dock where Commodore Robert E. DeNatale had organized a spectacular champagne and caviar reception. While Mark and I felt totally overwhelmed by the pomp and circumstance, we relished the moment." [68]

Roust, a Sea Sprite 34 sailed under celestial rules and double-handed
by Skipper Ian Gumprecht and Navigator Mark Swanson were first overall in the 2013 race.
Photo: Fran Grenon

Corinthian Resolve: The Story of the Marion-Bermuda Race

A double rainbow leads *Roust*, the overall winner in 2013, out of Buzzards Bay. Photo: Ian Gumprecht

MISCHIEVOUS

ABOVE: The two Massachusetts Maritime Academy entries in the 2015 race. *Spirit*, the red J44, was sailed by an all-women crew of cadets, while *Mischievous* had a mixed-gender crew. Photo: Fran Grenon

LEFT: The Massachusetts Maritime Academy won back-to-back elapsed time honors in 2013 and 2015. *Mischievous* is a Meriten 65 shown with a full complement of cadets starting the 2015 race. Photo: Fran Grenon

Ti was the overall winner in 2015. Skippered by Gregg Marston of Falmouth, Maine,
Ti was navigated using celestial methods by Andrew Howe and Chase Marston,
co-winners of the Navigator's Trophy. Photo: Fran Grenon

The 2015 Race

Oddly enough, the 2013 pattern was repeated in the 2015 Marion-Bermuda Race. Massachusetts Maritime Academy again entered a fast boat and again, they won line honors. *Mischievous* is a Meriten 65 donated to the MMA by Charles Cahill, was sailed by the cadets over the 645-mile course in 3 days, 5 hours and 12 minutes, second only to *Lilla*. This writer

watched her pass by at Sow & Pigs with the young sailors lining the windward rail, waving happily as they headed south southeast on a rhumb line course to Bermuda. The wind was a constant southwesterly, and the Gulf Stream particularly lumpy. Several boats had difficulty, but *Mischievous* was commanded well and sailed hard. The Massachusetts Maritime Academy was awarded the Blue Water Sailing

Corinthian Resolve: The Story of the Marion-Bermuda Race

Club Trophy for a second race in a row, beating *Shindig's* time by over 9 hours.

An Alden Mistral 36-footer named *Ti* from Falmouth, ME and just about the smallest boat in the fleet, won overall honors. Sailed by Greg Marston and members of his family, *Ti* also competed in the celestial class. Andrew Howe who guided *Ti* won the Navigator's Trophy for the best performance by a celestially-navigated yacht.

David Caso in *Silhouette*, the Cherubini 44, won class C honors. *Silhouette* is becoming one of the most decorated yachts in Marion-Bermuda history, including a first overall (2007), three first in class trophies, and three additional awards.

Two other events in 2015 stand out in the history of the race. One is that a sailor died while racing, although unlike the tragedy of Donald Hill's death in the 1989 race due to an injury suffered during an accidental jibe, in 2015 William Fasnacht of Mystic, CT died of natural causes aboard *Legacy V* when the yacht was about halfway to Bermuda. The Trustees, and all racers, recognized the loss with a memorial moment of silence at the awards ceremonies in Bermuda following the race.

The second event was that for the first time, the Bavier award for exemplary seamanship was awarded not for an act during the race. In 2015 the trophy and citation were awarded well after the fleet had returned to the US. The trophy went to *Sparky*, skipper Rob McAlpine and his crew for exceptional performance in helping a foundering yacht on the return trip. *Restive* is an Alden-designed beauty raced by George Denny in several Marion-Bermuda races. On the return trip from Bermuda in 2015 they lost their rudder. James G. Blaine, a member of that *Restive* return crew, wrote the following about the event:

"I had just gone below to get some sleep, leaving the others on deck to discuss lunch, when without

George Denny's Alden-designed 48-foot sloop *Restive* built in Brooklin, Maine has competed in several Marion-Bermuda races. On her return in 2015 she suffered a catastrophic rudder-post failure that forced an abandon ship. The crew of *Sparky* won the Bavier Trophy, for the first time awarded for exceptional seamanship on a return trip, as they rescued the *Restive* crew at sea. Photo: Fran Grenon

Restive at a quieter time in Center Harbor, Maine.
Photo: James G. Blaine

by the helmsman, but was being driven solely by the force of the waves. It was just a matter of time before the lower bearing failed, particularly in rough seas, and even I had figured out that when that happened, *Restive* would sink….

The seas were growing rougher. The once-distant line of squalls was now directly above us and seemed in no hurry to move on. Heavy rains fell, waves surged to 12 feet, and winds were gusting to 40 knots. George was on the radio trying to notify the Coast Guard and locate any nearby boats. David and Dave devised ever-more-ingenious efforts to stabilize the rudder, all of which failed." [69]

warning, the wheel, which was on autopilot, holding steadily to our north-by-northwest course, began rotating wildly. All efforts to steer manually failed, and we found ourselves adrift on an empty sea—140 miles from the closest dry land and several thousand feet above the ocean's floor. We hadn't seen another boat in 72 hours.

Restive proved her mettle by neatly heaving to into the wind, while the collective brainpower tried to figure out what to do. Clearly, the problem was the rudder, and so Dave descended into the bowels of the boat to have a look.

"I've found the problem," he called up from below, and as he scrambled back on deck, the once-distant squalls were closing in, the waves had swelled to over eight feet, and the wind was now blowing 20-30 knots.

"We have," Dave said, "a major structural failure."

Dry rot in the rudderpost had caused the upper bearing to fail. This made steering impossible because the rudder could no longer be controlled

George Denny put out a Mayday on VHF channel 16, and three yachts in the area responded, including *Sparky*, a Hinckley Sou'wester 42 skippered by Rob McAlpine. *Sparky* was seven miles ahead of *Restive* on their return trip, and immediately turned 180° to help. Aboard *Restive*, the skipper and crew discussed immediate options, given the expected hour or more it would take for *Sparky* to reach them. Denny considered those options, and decided to deploy the life raft as a contingency once *Sparky* hove into sight.

The raft was deployed off the stern. The crew found they were unable to bring the raft around to amidships where the boat's motion was less. They watched the waves, and one by one they jumped into the raft off *Restive's* bucking fantail. They timed their leaps when her stern was down to meet the next rising wave. Blaine wrote that one of his crewmates said, "For me, jumping into that raft was the most frightening part of the entire event. Not being able to jump without turning around and throwing myself backwards into where I hoped the raft would be was terrifying. A total leap of faith." They then cut the painter and drifted free of *Restive*.

Corinthian Resolve: The Story of the Marion-Bermuda Race

Sparky and her crew weren't unoccupied while this was happening. With Rob McAlpine directing matters, and Bob Kostyla at the helm, *Sparky* practiced the approach to the raft three times to make sure they got it right. They were under sail, recognizing that if they ran the engine, the prop could foul any one of the numerous lines dragging in the water, including the raft's severed painter. As they approached, *Sparky* threw the raft a line. The castaways tried to hold on to it, but couldn't. *Sparky* was moving too fast. They circled again. This time, except for Kostyla, McAlpine arranged the crew on the leeward rail. As they came around, they again tossed a line to the raft and every *Restive* crewman grabbed ahold of it or someone who had it, and the *Sparky* crew hauled the raft to the side of the pitching Hinckley. Everyone was manhandled aboard successfully. Skipper George Denny exited the raft last. There was only one wounded shin; proof they'd been dragged across *Sparky's* toerail. A salvage crew was deployed from the mainland, and with considerable difficulty, towed *Restive* in to Fairhaven, Massachusetts. She since has been repaired and is back in sailing trim.

On September 18, 2015 McAlpine, Kostyla, Denny and others involved in the rescue, as well as Marion-Bermuda Race Executive Director Allan McLean, several Trustees (including the author) and other club and race notables, met at the Beverly Yacht Club. McAlpine and the entire *Sparky* crew were awarded the Bavier Trophy for the 2015 race. It was the only time the Bavier has been awarded for the return trip. The deed of award reads: "Awarded by vote of the Race Committee in recognition of outstanding seamanship, Corinthian spirit or other special contribu-

tion to offshore sailing made during the Marion-Bermuda Race…" The award was well-deserved.

It also was obvious to all present that the two crews had become the closest of friends. This is what happens to sailors in the Marion-Bermuda Race. Whether forged through a rescue at sea, being thrashed by big seas and heavy wind offshore, or even collectively suffering through a mind-numbing and interminable calm, sailors who race from Marion to Bermuda, and who do so understanding that it's a race to be won as a Corinthian, friendship made will remain life-long. We are partners in an endeavor initially visualized by two good friends, perfected by hundreds of volunteers, and sustained by a very big and good idea—go to sea, sail fast, and win if it's your lot. Do so in your own boat under your own command with good friends doing their very best to win. Sail with Corinthian resolve.

A crewman is hoisted aloft aboard *Bermuda Oyster* to address a rigging issue. *Bermuda Oyster*, an Oyster 435 skippered by Paul Hubbard, was a frequent and often decorated Bermuda entry in the Marion-Bermuda Race.
Photo: Fran Grenon

Mischievous arriving in Bermuda waters after a fast passage in 2015. Photo: Fran Grenon

How to Win the Marion-Bermuda Race

In honor of the 10th Marion-Bermuda Race, Charlie Bascom wrote an article in the race book summarizing his interviews with three successful Marion-Bermuda sailors: Ron Noonan, the two-time overall winner (1983 and 1993) in *Wildflower*, Max Mehlburger who won in *Pirate* in 1985, and himself as navigator aboard John Cochran's *Sly Mongoose IV* in which he won back-to-back line honors in 1981 and 1983. The question addressed in the article is how to win the race. It's a valuable "How To" guide for anyone planning to give the race his or her best effort; not just get to Bermuda safely (which is, indeed, one of the good reasons to sail in Marion-Bermuda), but to get there first; either overall, or on corrected time. The article is worth quoting extensively.

Ron Noonan

Ron Noonan, the only repeat overall winner of Marion-Bermuda (as of this writing) said the following about his race strategy:

> "I divide the race into three segments, each of which requires a different strategy. The beat out of the bay…often is quite decisive…You use "around the buoys" strategies going down the Bay, watching the currents and the wind, and there are geological shifts as well. Almost everybody ends up playing the shores, but it's not automatic.

The second segment is from the Sow and Pigs to the Stream Here, you're trying to enter the Stream at the proper point and also cash in on any eddies you encounter along the way…

The third segment runs from your exit from the Stream to the finish. This is 60 percent of the race. Projecting what the wind is going to do and how to take advantage of it are the skills for this segment.

When you're inside the 50-mile mark, going for the barn is a very strong temptation, but it's been my experience that when you get close to Bermuda, the wind generally backs to the south-southwest, so it's often wise to keep some windward money in the bank…

My favorite number of people [aboard] is six, made up of the navigator, who doesn't stand watch, two permanent watch captains, and three crew. The crew rotates so that one crew member is off-duty for 24 hours. The off-duty does all the housekeeping, cooking, cleanup, and so forth, and is first call on any "evolution," such as a reef or a sail change. The second call is the navigator and third is the off-watch.

We run six hour watches during the day, 6 am to noon, noon to 6 pm and then four hour watches through the night. That way, we can get a good five hours in the sack and be really rested, and the system is self-dogging. Because sunrise is about 4:30, there's only one black watch, from 10 pm until 2 am."

Max Mehlburger

Charlie Bascom also interviewed Max Mehlburger, skipper of *Pirate*, a Swan 38 that won overall in 1985. Mehlburger hailed from Little Rock, Arkansas. Bascom asked him how he knew he'd done well approaching the finish line in that race:

"The first indication that we'd maybe done well was when we heard Herb Marcus [*Silkie*], a Tartan 41 in Class C, make the VHF call to the Finish Line Committee. I remember thinking that we must be doing pretty good if we're that close to Herb…

Pirate was ninth across the finish, just after 7am. The wind was howling, so we pulled into St. George's and rafted up beside a Swan 48, with none other than William Hurt on board. Hurt delivered this soliloquy to his own shipmates: "Now look at this little 38-footer. These guys did it right—this is the way you're supposed to do it…"

You see, most boats stayed close to the rhumb, whereas we were rather radical. My navigator, Nick Nicholson, and I listened carefully to the weather forecasts, talked it over, and—I know this sounds crazy—we went 110 miles west of the rhumb line…The wind shift was about 24 hours behind schedule and we were wringing our hands, but finally it veered and there we were, windward of the fleet. The poor guys on the rhumb had it right on the nose. Then the wind came up. We were on a beam reach and we all took turns seeing who could make the boat go fastest. There were times when *Pirate* was surfing at 14 or more, down the face of the waves, all day long. That's really how the race was won."

According to Jack Braitmayer's log, that wind shift reached most of the fleet at 1730 on Tuesday June 25, and it came in at 25 knots. Located 110 miles to the west, Mehlburger must have picked up the shift five hours earlier, and in a windward position. In retrospect, it's clear how *Pirate* won silver that year.

Charlie Bascom

Finally, in the 1995 race book article, Bascom told his own story of how to win. In 1981 and 1983 he was navigator aboard the back-to-back first to finish yacht *Sly Mongoose IV* owned by John Cochran. Bascom wrote:

"First to Finish is totally different.

For the past decade, the race's First Overall winner has typically been a yacht from class E, F or G. So, if you're on a big class A number, your chances of First Overall are dim at best. Your better bets are First to Finish and First in Class.

The notion of being First to Finish grows quietly, like a plant. Superstition makes it a forbidden topic, but you can tell it's on the crew's mind. They're all scanning the horizon and repeatedly asking about your position. They want to know if you've heard any radio chatter from the other big boats. A mild tension creeps into everyone on board and time seems to slow down.

Every racing yacht must hail the Finish Line Committee on VHF radio when about five miles out. If you think you have a shot at First to Finish, you will spend the last forty miles of the race on pins and needles, listening to emptiness on the VHF. What you don't want to hear is any other racing yacht making that radio call before you do.

Someone will suggest turning off the VHF but you can't. You can't set yourself up to think you

may have won it and not know that someone else took it away. You've got to stay glued to channel 72 for the duration…

With twenty miles to go, the island is staring right at you and you'll find you can't stand it any longer. Always have some young people aboard, people who will stay cheerful when you tell them that, despite the heel angle, you're going to crank them to the mast top with big binoculars so they can reconnoiter the horizon for competitors. This is an extremely high pressure exercise because within minutes, either they're going to yell down to you that there's a sail well ahead and the trophy's gone, or they're going to yell down to you that you're number one.

With five miles to go, you make your first VHF call to the Finish Line Committee. Now the shoe's on the other foot, you reflect—how many other racers' hopes just popped like soap bubbles?…You pass by the finish buoys and, after the longest thirty seconds in the race, the "Welcome to Bermuda" greeting comes in over the VHF. You'd think it was the final point at Wimbledon. The entire crew shrieks and runs around the deck congratulating each other… An enormous serenity descends and you find yourself sitting down somewhere, breathing deeply with your eyes closed. It's like letting air out of a balloon…The press is there, zooming around your boat, getting you and shooting rolls of film… Some serious refreshments appear."

According to Noonan, Mehlburger, and Bascom, that's how you win the Marion-Bermuda Race, and that's how it feels to do so.[70]

Anne Kolker and her all-women crew aboard *Etoile* off to a fast start in the 2011 Marion-Bermuda Race. Photo: Fran Grenon

Corinthian Resolve: The Story of the Marion-Bermuda Race

Afterword

After five years of conceiving, designing, promoting, planning, administering and documenting a major new ocean race, David and Trudy Kingery were exhausted. It was Monday the 13th of June, 1977 and time for them to drive the 75 miles southeastward across Massachusetts. They were on their way from their winter home in Cambridge down to Marion to help bring order to the pre-start chaos of the inaugural Marion-Bermuda Race.

Dave could never hide from his well-deserved reputation as a quant. After all, he was a tenured Professor at MIT. Among other duties, he had agreed to create the scratch sheet for this first race. Dave was talented, but like everyone else involved with Marion-Bermuda, was a volunteer. He had professional access to the most powerful computers in the world, but this was well before the days of the PC and distributed data processing. So, he worked hours, on evenings and weekends, to set up and calculate classes and handicap ratings for each of the entries. He did it all by hand.

He and Dickie Bird had expected 30, maybe 40 boats to show up. Most considered even these numbers wildly optimistic for a first-time yacht race. When the 100th registration came in, he and Dickie both felt a little queasy. They allowed themselves the smug satisfaction of finally knowing for sure that they'd tapped into a major opportunity for an ocean race of the type they believed the sport was missing. But they simultaneously wondered how they could handle such a large number of entries? It was three times the number of boats they'd expected. On a more practical level, how on Earth could Dave calculate handicaps for such a large, and stunningly diverse, race fleet? How could

they, with their limited volunteer crew, handle the start, safely monitor fleet progress, and deal with the crowds at the Bermuda receptions? Furthermore, both Kingery and Bird planned to sail their own boats in the race. Not only did they organize the race, they organized themselves, their boats and their crews to make the 645-mile fast passage, as well as the trip home.

Kingery and Bird decided it must stop, and closed registration at the 110th boat. Trudy helped type up the scratch sheets, and Dave had them copied. They loaded the boxes of paper into their conspicuous 1975 powder blue Mustang with a convertible top, the kind of car collectors covet these days. They stopped for dinner in Boston's North End with their Blue Water Sailing Club friends Shirley and Jack Roberts.

On that Monday evening in 1977, Kingerys somehow found parking and joined their friends for dinner at a Hanover Street Italian favorite. When they later returned to the spot where they'd parked the blue convertible loaded with hand-calculated scratch sheets, the car was gone. It had been stolen.

Dave and Trudy Kingery did what any couple would do: they stood stunned and open-mouthed. In an interview, Trudy couldn't remember what exactly happened next. It's unclear whether she and Dave were more concerned about the car, or the scratch sheets for the inaugural ocean race for more than 100 yachts about to get underway in Marion. She does recall that after reporting the theft, she and Dave somehow got home to Cambridge (presumably with the help of their dinner companions), and they got right back to work. All night, Dave labored to recalculate

Corinthian Resolve: The Story of the Marion-Bermuda Race

and recreate the scratch sheets for the 110-boat fleet. This race had been in the planning stages since 1972 when the Kingerys and Birds first met at the RHADC dock in Hamilton, Bermuda. Losing all the critical documents days before the start wasn't about to faze them.

They got the job done, and again with the help of their friends, Dave and Trudy arrived in Marion the next day, exhausted once more, but undoubtedly happy to gaze out on Sippican Harbor off Marion. Ocean-capable sailing yachts swung at nearly every mooring. Spray cloths with sail numbers were being rigged. The harbor was filling up with competitors preparing for the start of a new, and very different yacht race that would set the standard for what a great Corinthian ocean race should be.

As a retired Royal naval officer and aviator, Bird felt comfortable on the ocean, and certainly with the navigation and seamanship challenges posed by the featureless oceanic distances between Bermuda and New England. He loved his *Water Gypsy* and liked sailing the Bermuda-blue waters around his island. However, Bird never completed a Marion-Bermuda Race. He entered *Water Gypsy* in the inaugural race, was fouled at the starting line, and that was it. He never entered his yacht in another one.

Kingery was very different from Bird. Kingery has been difficult for this author to get to know. His was a far more opaque personality. However, one can well imagine that while Bird enjoyed the start and finish, Kingery was more at home on the actual voyage. He was happiest at sea. He enjoyed solitude. His favorite one-design, the International 110, is typically sailed singlehanded. He was taciturn and reflective. He was far more analytical and organized than

most. He was technically brilliant, and as brilliant people often are, particularly when at the apex of their field, Kingery was more prone to command than coddle.

On the RHADC dock in 1972 two men met and the Marion-Bermuda Race was conceived of. One, a gregarious Royal Navy aviator transplanted to Bermuda, the other an analytical tactical genius from MIT. One could hand-calculate yacht racing handicaps and solve complicated technical problems; the other could motivate volunteer spirits and throw a great party. All are necessary ingredients in organizing a premier yacht race.

The Marion-Bermuda Race went on to great success. By now hundreds of yachts and thousands of sailors have participated in over forty years of racing. The themes from the historical record of these races are clear: the Marion-Bermuda Race is first and foremost a Corinthian race. Skippers sail their own boats for the fun of it with all-amateur crews, many of them family members. Simultaneously, strict entry criteria, yacht inspections, seamanship training, and mentoring are in the fabric of the Marion-Bermuda Race as well. These make the passage across the Gulf Stream safer and more practical. Accidents have and will continue to happen, but Marion-Bermuda sailors are as well-prepared as anyone to meet the challenges of three or four days at sea out of sight of land beyond the reach of rapid search and rescue.

The Marion-Bermuda Race will continue as a cornerstone event in North Atlantic yacht racing. The race's underlying principles will be adhered to, both because they attract good sailors, but also because the race organizers and competitors know that they are important to sustain. The future of the Marion-Bermuda Race is bright. David Kingery and Dickie Bird wouldn't be the least bit surprised.

Her Majesty Queen Elizabeth II visited the Dinghy Club in November, 1955. She reconfirmed the "Royal" grant to the RHADC, and christened the club's new fitted dinghy *Elizabeth II*. Photo: RHADC Archives

The Hinckley Pilot 35 *Panacea* on her way to Bermuda in 2005.
She would be the overall winner. Photo: Fran Grenon

Corinthian Resolve: The Story of the Marion-Bermuda Race

Acknowledgments

The number of people who have willingly and freely made significant contributions to this story is humbling. The following is a partial listing, and to any I've forgotten, your omission is entirely my fault.

In Bermuda, Jean Bird met me at the airport, transported me around her island, welcomed me into her home, and hosted me for lunches at the Dinghy Club and at the Royal Bermuda Yacht Club. Through her anecdotes, clippings, files, artifacts and records I got to know Dickie Bird whom I never had the chance to meet in person. Jean is a very special person and a good friend.

Former RHADC Commodore Buddy Rego shared his own stories, but also arranged a series of meetings and conversations with Bermudians who currently are involved with the race, and central to its success in the past and present. John Carey made sure that I heard the great yarns about *Satan's Mercy* as well as other not-so-serious events, and like Buddy, introduced me to important Bermudians who helped me document this story. Another recent Commodore, Allan Williams, was a profoundly important contributor, to both the history of the race, as well as the history of the RHADC itself. As mentioned here, his father, H.L. Williams, was Commodore in the mid-1960s and made sure the RHADC bought the Mangroville mansion in Paget which it now occupies with its splendid marina and harbor views. Allan also arranged for me to meet with Eugene Rayner, the Bermudian who until recently coordinated the finish line operation at St. David's which is one reason why for so many years and for so many races, whether from Newport, Marion, or elsewhere, Bermuda has been a favorite destination.

I am deeply indebted to Charles Dunstan, another former RHADC Commodore, and his wife Janis, for housing me on my two visits to Bermuda in late 2015 and early 2016 during research and archival combing. Charles and Janis also shuttled me about, and introduced me to people who had perspectives to share. They made me feel at home, both in their lovely waterside house, and at the Dinghy Club. Charles also agreed to be an early reviewer of this manuscript to help cleanse it of bone-headed mistakes made by any writer, but particularly this one, in early drafts. Thank you to Charles and Janis.

Neil Redburn was RHADC Vice Commodore while research and writing were underway, and not only had Marion-Bermuda stories of his own, but also switched me on to the Bermuda fitted dinghy. It is a wonderful boat, massively impractical, but such an integral part of amateur sailing in Bermuda and the RHADC that I had to include it here. Neil introduced me to Simon Jones at *The Royal Gazette* who helped me access important newspaper archives. Neil also walked me and Ray Cullum in to meet with Patricia Phillip-Fairn of the Bermuda Tourism office whose infectious enthusiasm for Bermuda, the Marion-Bermuda Race, and for this book project, will help secure their success.

I want to thank members of the Warren Brown family who sent photos and fact-checked me on *War Baby*, including the origins of the yacht's name. Warren Brown was a great amateur racing sailor, and *War Baby* continued winning long after Ted Turner had turned her over to this prominent Bermudian.

I extend thanks to Ed Faries, RHADC Commodore while research for the book was underway. Ed made all the

Spirit of Bermuda at the start of the 2015 race.
Spirit is Bermuda's national tall ship.
Photo: Fran Grenon

resources and facilities of the club available to me as I worked to sort through and understand the musty files. He put the Club's "Snooker Room" at my disposal. I could spread documents and files out across the entire (covered) playing surface, although that was much to the chagrin of the snooker players at the club. To Ed, and to Ross Spurling and the rest of the RHADC snooker enthusiasts, I send my thanks.

I will never forget Ed's wife Cathy who talked me into being guest speaker at the annual RHADC ladies luncheon while I was at work there in December, 2015. I had no idea that I would be a (very poor) substitute for the Governor's wife Martha Fergusson who was called home to the UK on a family emergency the day before the luncheon. I dutifully gave a talk on my prior book about nineteenth century America's Cup sailors from Deer Isle, Maine, something that I am certain held no interest for the women gathered for the event. Only afterwards did I discover the real reason I held their attention for 30 minutes. I had been the first, and only, male guest speaker at that venerable RHADC event. I had broken the glass ceiling!

Finally, in Bermuda, I want to especially thank Wendy Augustus, Secretary at the Dinghy Club. She arranged to haul out of dusty storage box after moldy box of records stretching back to 1977 and earlier. Files don't store well in the ocean air of Bermuda, so this task wasn't trivial. Wendy also provided me with all the logistics support I needed while working in the snooker room. I was well cared for; thank you Wendy.

In Marion, Alan Minard and Nan Johnson are directly or indirectly responsible for much of this book. They sorted through and opened race archives. They introduced me to and accompanied me on visits with local people who have been involved with the race since the beginning, like Charles and Faith Paulsen. Nan organized the four Executive Assistants to get together for the first time in many years for a photograph, an important addition to

Four Marion-Bermuda Race Executive/Administrative Secretaries at the Beverly Yacht Club in Marion in 2016. Left to right: Annette Hodess (1987); Trudy Kingery (1981-1985); Faith Paulsen (1989-2003); and Nan Johnson (2007-Present). Photo: Christine Dole

the historical record. This book wouldn't have happened without Alan and Nan.

Trudy Kingery got me started on all of this. Immediately after Allan McLean gave me this assignment, I and my wife Betsy visited Trudy in her home in Marion village. She was flattered we came, but it was instantly clear that she was the most knowledgeable of sources for the early years of the Marion-Bermuda Race. I returned to meet with Trudy again, to fact-check some of the things I'd learned in Bermuda, and she was gracious and helpful again.

Jack and Nancy Braitmayer also deserve special thanks. Jack is a towering figure in the history of the Marion-Bermuda Race. He has sailed it seven times, and has a near-perfect memory of each race. In addition, his logbooks are astonishing. In all my years, I never have seen anything like them. They are complete, organized, and bound chronologically. The history of those seven races, day by day, watch by watch, 30 minutes by 30 minutes, is all there. Jack treasures these books, and he allowed me to remove them from his home overlooking Sippican Harbor

Corinthian Resolve: The Story of the Marion-Bermuda Race

so that I could examine them. This book became as much a story of ocean racing, as it is of an ocean race, largely because of Jack, Nancy and their *Karina* logs.

My good friends Paul and Annette Hoddess have homes in Marion and Cambridge, and are members of both the Beverly Yacht Club and Blue Water Sailing Club. Paul is a veteran of multiple Marion-Bermuda Races. and has been involved in its management. Annette served as Executive Secretary when the race reached its peak participation levels of over 160 yachts in the late 1980s. Paul and Annette shared stories, showed me personal photographs of the races and receptions, and helped me sort myth from reality.

Also in Marion, Ray Cullum has worked tirelessly on behalf of this project, helping me get it off the ground in the first place, sourcing photographs from the race archives and his and his wife Wendy's personal collections, as well as other local sources. Like Charles Dunstan, Ray kindly agreed to give this manuscript a once-over to make sure it didn't misrepresent anything, although I continue to say that any errors and omissions are my own. Ray and Wendy are great friends and strong supporters of the race and this project.

In Boston, I must thank Joe and Rhoda Fantasia who met with me on the waterfront and shared their recollections about the early days of the race, and in particular, told me about Dave Kingery and Dickie Bird. They also had tapes of some early documentaries of the race they gave me for review. Through these I heard and saw Dave Kingery on the screen, and vicariously sailed with Geraldo Rivera and other racers in the early 1980s.

Jack Westerbeke shared photos and stories of his races in *Isolde*. Jack and Cil Westerbeke are active members of the Blue Water Sailing Club, Jack was Commodore when the race was reaching its highest points in the 1980s. Their support of the book project has been important, particularly in the early stages.

Many of the photos in the book are from Fran Grenon of Spectrum Photography. Fran has been photographing the race since 2003. The quality of his work is self-evident, but his willingness to both organize and make easily accessible his library of hundreds and hundreds of images has made writing this book far more enjoyable, and a better history.

Allan McLean, currently Executive Director of the Marion-Bermuda race, got me into this, and for that I am grateful. Allan is a great sailor and good friend. He also runs a great ocean race.

In New York, I thank Vanessa Cameron at the New York Yacht Club, the home of one of the nation's great yachting history libraries. I did most of my research in secondary sources like *SAIL* magazine and *Yachting* in the 44th Street library, and Vanessa was a great help as always.

John Rousmaniere is perhaps our leading yachting historian. He helped in the early, middle, and final stages of this project. He read the manuscript and helped me smoke out important errors of fact and emphasis. He also was congratulatory and enthusiastic about the book, which means more to me than he'll ever know. He felt well enough about the book to write an insightful Foreword, and for these things, I am very grateful to John.

My daughter Lisa Gabrielson McCurdy also gave the manuscript a close read. She is my best and most highly-qualified critic. As of this writing she is on the editorial team at *Sailing World* magazine. She has a sharp and well-informed eye for sailing narrative and language. Her edits have improved the writing immensely.

Above all, I thank my wife Betsy. She always supports what I do, even if I don't do it particularly well. Because of her I am the luckiest guy around. It also helps that she loves to sail…

Mark J. Gabrielson
Boston, MA.

FIRST OVERALL

FIRST-TO-FINISH

BAVIER

FAMILY

FIRST ALL-WOMEN CREW

FIRST SERVICE ACADEMY

Appendix A: Marion-Bermuda Race Selected Trophy Winners

1977

Overall	*Silkie*	H. Marcus
First-to-Finish	*Silkie*	H. Marcus
Shorthanded	*Silkie*	H. Marcus
Navigator		H. Marcus

1979

Overall	*Gabriella*	H. Clayman
First-to-Finish	*Gabriella*	H. Clayman
Shorthanded	*Astri*	W. Foss
Family	*Asteroid*	A. Doughty, Sr.
Navigator		J. Clayman
Bavier		W. D. Kingery

1981

Overall	*Edelweiss*	A. Shatkin
First-to-Finish	*Sly Mongoose IV*	J. Cochran
Shorthanded	*Silkie*	H. Marcus
Family	*Legend*	K. Carse, Sr.
Navigator		N. Nicholson
Bavier		R. Biebel and crew

1983

Overall	*Pirate*	M. Mehlburger
First-to-Finish	*Sly Mongoose IV*	J. Cochran
Shorthanded	*Silkie*	H. Marcus
Family	*Asteroid*	A. Doughty, Sr.
Navigator		D. Jones
Bavier		Not awarded

1985

Overall	*Pirate*	M. Mehlburger
First-to-Finish	*Charisma*	R. Beres
Shorthanded	*Silkie*	H. Marcus
Family	*Legend*	K. Carse, Sr.
Navigator		N. Nicholson
Bavier		T. Warner and P. Kenney, and Air Sea Rescue, U.S. Naval Station Bermuda

1987

Overall	*Legend*	K. Carse, Sr.
First-to-Finish	*Runaway*	P. D'Arcy
Shorthanded	*Astri*	W. Foss
Family	*Legend*	K. Carse, Sr.
Navigator		K. Carse, Sr.
Bavier		P. Nelson

1989

Overall	*Yukon Jack*	J. Elliott
First-to-Finish	*War Baby*	W. A. Brown
Shorthanded	*Yukon Jack*	J. Elliott
Family	*Wind's Way*	S. and J. McFarlane
Navigator		T. Plummer
Bavier		Not awarded

1991

Overall	*Orion*	R. Carelton
First-to-Finish	*Alphida*	E. K. Cooper
Shorthanded	*Aequoreal II*	P. Rasmussen
Family	*Sinn Fein*	P. Rebovich
Navigator		R. Norton
Bavier		F. Checkoski

1993

Overall	*Wildflower*	R. Noonan
First-to-Finish	*Alphida*	E. K. Cooper
Shorthanded	*Xapiema*	R. Walsh
Family	*Karina*	J. Braitmayer
Navigator		R. Norton and K. Reed
Bavier		Not awarded

1995

Overall	*Kemancha*	C. Cordner
First-to-Finish	*Columbine*	R. Leather
Shorthanded	*Shooting Star*	D. Kingsbury
Family	*Xapiema*	R. Walsh
Navigator		J. Hackett
Bavier		Not awarded

1997

Overall	*Majek*	A. Fletcher
First-to-Finish	*AKKA*	A. Rosenbladt
Shorthanded	*Next Boat*	M. Ellman
Family	*Impala*	A. Sanford
Navigator		M. Fletcher
Bavier		Not awarded

1999

Overall	*Dakota*	D. Ely
First-to-Finish	*Temptress*	R. Shulman
Shorthanded	*Rocinante*	D. Ritchie
Family	*Althea*	W. Ewing III
Navigator		Midshipman G. Mitchell
Bavier		Not awarded

Corinthian Resolve: The Story of the Marion-Bermuda Race

2001

Overall	*Spinache*	J. Lawless
First-to-Finish	*Veritas*	P. Hutchinson
Shorthanded	*Panacea* (Celestial) *Rhapsody* (Electronic)	G. MacDonald M. Asaro
Family	*Rhapsody*	M. Asaro
Navigator		R. Graham
Bavier		Not awarded

2003

Overall	*Gorgeous Girl*	G. Jones
First-to-Finish	*Starr Trail*	R. Mulderig
Shorthanded	*Dark Lady*	D. Gibbons
Family	*Wischbone*	J. Wisch
Navigator		G. Greenwald
Bavier		D. Roblin

2005

Overall	*Panacea*	G. MacDonald
First-to-Finish	*Mameluke*	G. Storer
Shorthanded	*Panacea*	G. MacDonald
Family	*Maki*	J. White
Navigator		W. Taylor
All Female	*Panama Red*	R. Bioty
Bavier		J. Mollicone

2007

Overall	*Silhouette*	D. Caso
First-to-Finish	*Morgan's Ghost*	P. Hutchins
Shorthanded	*Avalon*	A. Feldman
Family	*Four Stars*	T. McAdams
Navigator		W. Lacey
Bavier		Not awarded

2009

Overall	*Crescendo*	M. Jacobson
First-to-Finish	*Crescendo*	M. Jacobson
Shorthanded	*Windsong II*	L. Roberts
Family		Not awarded
Navigator		J. Whitty
Bavier		Not awarded

2011

Overall	*Lilla*	S. De Pietro
First-to-Finish	*Lilla*	S. De Pietro
Shorthanded	*Corsair*	A. Risch
Family	*Meridian*	M. Beach
Navigator		L. Hall
All Female	*Etoile*	A. Kolker
Bavier		Not awarded

2013

Overall	*Roust*	I. Gumprecht
First-to-Finish	*Shindig*	M. Reney
Shorthanded	*Attitude*	S. Dahlen
Family	*Seaquester*	R. McLaughlin, Jr.
Navigator		R. Wisner
All Female	*Etoile*	A. Kolker
Bavier		Not awarded

2015

Overall	*Ti*	G. Marston
First-to-Finish	*Mischievous*	A. Cahill
Shorthanded	*Trust Me*	J. Dowling
Family	*Ti*	G. Marston
Navigator		A. Howe and C. Marston
All Female	*Etoile*	A. Kolker
Bavier		R. McAlpine and the crew of *Sparky*

Marion Bermuda Cruising Yacht Race

Family Fun Race & Gosling's Party

Awards Ceremony at Governor's Mansion

Flag Lowering Ceremonies

Golf Outing

A 2007 collage showing the Bermuda events arranged by the RHADC
for Marion-Bermuda participants upon their arrival in Bermuda.
Source: RHADC Archives

Appendix B: Marion-Bermuda Race Handicap Systems

Race Year	Handicap System
1977	New England Yacht Racing Rule (NER). No spinnakers
1979	NER with "Special Coefficient" for mast height. No spinnakers
1981	NER with "Special Coefficient" for mast height. No spinnakers
1983	US Yacht Racing Union MHS—cruising canvas. No spinnakers
1985	USYRU MHS—cruising canvas. No spinnakers
1987	Marion-Bermuda Race Handicap System. No spinnakers
1989	MBRHS. No spinnakers
1991	MBRHS. No spinnakers
1993	MBRHS. No spinnakers
1995	MBRHS. No spinnakers
1997	International Measurement System. No spinnakers
1999	US Sailing AmeriCap. No spinnakers
2001	US Sailing AmeriCap. No spinnakers
2003	US Sailing AmeriCap II. No poled spinnakers
2005	US Sailing AmeriCap II. No poled spinnakers
2007	Offshore Racing Rule 2007. No poled spinnakers
2009	ORR. No poled spinnakers
2011	ORR. No poled spinnakers. IRC if 6 or more boats entered as IRC yachts
2013	Founders Division: ORR. Big Yachts (65'-100'): ORR. Classic Yachts: ASTA. Spinnakers
2015	Founders Division: ORR. Big Yachts (65'-100'): ORR. Classic Yachts: ASTA. Spinnakers

Shindig lifts her forward sections clear of the water as she approaches hull speed at the start of the 2013 race.
Manned by Massachusetts Maritime Academy cadets, *Shindig* would be first across the line
and win the Blue Water Sailing Club Commodore's Cup in the 2013 Marion-Bermuda Race. Photo: Fran Grenon

Endnotes

[1] I am indebted to Jack and Nancy Braitmayer for sharing with me their stories and perspectives, as well as the complete set of *Karina* log books that cover Jack's seven races: 1979, 1981, 1985, 1987, 1989, 1991, and 1993. As a US Air Force-trained weather observer, Jack's meteorological entries are particularly valuable records of conditions during those seven races.

[2] Fox, Robin Lane. *The Classical World: An Epic History from Homer to Hadrian*. Basic Books, London, 2006. 35-40

[3] Rousmaniere, John. "Corinthian." Scuttlebutt. 2007.

[4] Roosevelt. P. James. "A Short History." www.seawanhaka.org. Accessed August 1, 2016.

[5] Rousmaniere, John. *Fastnet, Force 10*. W. W. Norton, New York. 1980 and 2000. 5

[6] I am deeply grateful to Jean Middleton Bird, Dickie Bird's widow and wife of 25 years, for providing full and unencumbered access to Dickie's files, correspondence, and mementos. Jean Bird is herself a larger-than-life personality showing all evidence of still adoring her late husband. She is among Bermuda's true treasures. Jean has led a noteworthy life of her own in Ceylon (Sri Lanka), Kenya, Tanzania, and finally with Dickie in Bermuda once they were married in 1985.

[7] I also am indebted to Trudy Kingery, David Kingery's wife of many years. The last of the original foursome (the Kingerys and Birds), over several interviews Trudy generously shared her memories of the early conversations among the four on the dock at the RHADC in 1972, and of the early races which she was central to organizing. She provided photos of *Keramos* and verified that Dickie's personal memo is an accurate summary of the race origins. Among other pursuits, Trudy now orchestrates the annual Buzzards Bay Musicfest from her home in Marion village.

[8] Rousmaniere, John. Private correspondence. November 21, 2016.

[9] Bavier, Bob. "From the Cockpit." *Yachting*. October, 1976. 56

[10] *The Royal Gazette*, August 19, 1976

[11] Rousmaniere, John. *A Berth to Bermuda*. Mystic Seaport Press. 2006. The first race from the US to Bermuda started off Brooklyn, NY in 1906. Subsequent races started off Brooklyn, Marblehead, Mass, New London, Conn., and Montauk, N.Y. before the start was moved permanently to Newport, R.I. in 1936. Held in even-numbered years, the race has been sailed 50 times through 2016.

[12] Payne, Bob. "Three races to the Onion Patch: The Bermuda Alternative." *SAIL*. September, 1977. 109

[13] Details of Dickie's life were provided by Jean Bird, several his Bermuda colleagues at the RHADC, as well as public sources, including an obituary published in *The Royal Gazette*, April 1, 2011.

[14] Details of David Kingery's life are based on his obituary published in *The New York Times*, July 8, 2000, *MIT News*, September, 1999, the *American Ceramic Society Newsletter*, September 16, 2015, interviews with

Trudy Kingery in December, 2015 and June, 2016, and an interview with his close friends and Marion-Bermuda collaborators Joe and Rhoda Fantasia in January, 2016.

[15] Gibbs, Tony. "Bermuda Cruising Race." *Yachting*. October, 1977. 194

[16] Payne, Bob. Ibid. 110

[17] "Race Circular, Blue Water Cruising Race, Marion-Bermuda." June 25, 1977. Section 1.9

[18] Payne, Bob. Ibid. 110

[19] Payne, Bob. Ibid. 111

[20] This brief history of the RHADC is drawn from several documents and interviews. Most importantly, a document titled "Royal Hamilton Amateur Dinghy Club: 130th Anniversary—September, 2012" held in the RHADC Archives, as well as conversations with former Commodores Allan Williams, Buddy Rego and John Carey in Bermuda.

[21] I am indebted to David Kettner who assembled a comprehensive history of the Blue Water Sailing Club in celebration of the 50th anniversary of its founding: *The First Fifty Years: 1959-2009*. Self-published by BWSC, 2009.

[22] "Cross Currents". *Yachting*. May, 1979. 24

[23] *The Royal Gazette*. 1995

[24] "Special Report to the Race Committee." September 21,1979. RHADC Archives

[25] "Report of Dismasting, CRESCENDO II, Marion/Bermuda Race, 7/4/79, Bermuda". RHADC Archives

[26] "Cross Currents." *Yachting*. September, 1979. 22

[27] *Boston Globe*. June 17, 1979. 82

[28] *SAIL*. August, 1979. 22.

[29] Fantasia, Joseph. Letter addressed to Edward Brainard II dated February 20, 1979. RHADC Archives

[30] Press release "Second Marion-Bermuda Race Set for June 22, 1979" Hamilton, Bermuda, August 30, 1978. RHADC Archives

[31] Herrington probably was paraphrasing Euripides in *The Herclidae*.

[32] This story of *Satan's Mercy* and her loss is based on several sources. James Holechek wrote an excellent article published in the *Baltimore Sun* July 26, 1981 for which he interviewed Herrington and Bill Boykin, a member of the crew and long-time sailing partner of Herrington's. Marcia Murphy of the *Day* wrote an article that was included in the 1983 Marion-Bermuda Race Book based on interviews with Boykin, crewmate Rob Pennington, and reports from the U.S. Coast Guard. She did not include Herrington. John Ahern published a story in the *Boston Globe* June 27, 1981 based on Herrington's verbal report to the Race Committee immediately after the finish.

[33] Holechek, James. *Baltimore Sun*. July 26, 1981. H2

[34] "Marion-Bermuda Cruising Race: A Beat to Bermuda". *SAIL*. September, 1981. 100

[35] The history of the Beverly Yacht Club is drawn from Rosbe, Judith Westlund, *The Beverly Yacht Club*, an Images of America publication. Arcadia Publishing Charleston, SC, 2006.

[36] Rousmaniere, John. Private correspondence. November 21, 2016.

[37] *SAIL*. September, 1983. 146B

[38] *SAIL*. September, 1985. 154B

[39] Marion-Bermuda website, accessed June 26, 2015. www.marionbermuda.com.

[40] *SAIL*. September, 1987. 106D

41 *Sailing World*. "Captain Outrageous". April 24, 2002

42 *Royal Gazette*. December 27, 2014

43 Rives Potts. Email to the author dated December 29, 2015

44 Line honors have gone to Bermuda boats *War Baby* (1989; course record), *Alphida* (1991 and 1993; course record), *Starr Trail* (2003); and *Morgan's Ghost* (2007).

45 *SAIL*. September, 1989. 65

46 Report filed by S.J. Peerless, M.D. addressed to Thomas H. Farquhar, Race Committee Chairman. July 3, 1989. RHADC Archives

47 Marion-Bermuda Race Book. 1979. 25

48 *Log*. A publication of the Blue Water Sailing Club. Spring 1977. 4

49 In 1983, '85, '87, and '89 Marion-Bermuda starting fleet sizes were 127, 128, 149, and 163. The Newport to Bermuda fleets in 1984, '86, '88, and '90 were 115, 125, 120, and 145.

50 *SAIL*. October, 1991. 110E

51 Letter from the Race Chairman to a competitor. July 3, 1991. RHADC Archives

52 *SAIL*. September, 1993. 98G

53 Interview with Eugene Rayner, February 10, 2016 at RHADC

54 Aero-News.Net. Accessed February 9, 2016

55 *SAIL*. October, 1997. 63

56 *The Royal Gazette*. June 8, 1999. 21

57 Bioty, Rebecca ("Becky"). Marion-Bermuda Race Book. 2007. 11

58 Gabrielson, Lisa. Private correspondence. November 22, 2016

59 Letter from John Carey to yacht *Heartsease Laurus Roc*. June 23, 2005. RHADC Archives

60 Cullum, Ray. Private correspondence. November 19, 2016

61 Marion-Bermuda Race Book. 2009. 5

62 Marion-Bermuda Race Book. 2011. 35

63 RHADC plaque. Transcribed February, 2015

64 *The Royal Gazette*. 1914. Sourced from a draft manuscript (incomplete) of a history of the Bermuda fitted dinghy, RHADC Archives

65 Marion Bermuda Race Book. 2013. 13

66 www.bermudasloop.org. Accessed November, 2016

67 Marion-Bermuda Race Book. 2015. 37

68 Marion-Bermuda Race Book. 2015. 25

69 Blaine, James G. "Rescue at Sea." Manuscript. Marion-Bermuda Race Archives

70 Marion-Bermuda Race Book. 1995. "In the Silver; Recollections of Some Winners." Charlie Bascom. 33

Jonathan Brewin's J160 *Big Bear*
in the Class A start to the stormy
2009 Marion-Bermuda Race.
Photo: Fran Grenon

A Friends and Family race is one of the fun events in Bermuda after the serious racing is done.
Here a competitor in the 2005 event puts everyone on the rail, mostly for the view. Photo: Fran Grenon

Corinthian Resolve: The Story of the Marion-Bermuda Race

Index

Corinthian Resolve: The Story of the Marion-Bermuda Race

Navigator Mark Swanson taking a sun sight aboard *Roust*,
Ian Gumprecht's Sea Sprite 34 that won the 2013 Marion-Bermuda Race.
Photo: Ian Gumprecht

A pair of Class B entries working their way
out of Buzzards Bay to start the 2005 race.
Photo: Fran Grenon

A view of the RHADC marina as competitors dress ship
following the 2013 Marion-Bermuda Race.
Photo: Ray Cullum